THE HOME SEWER'S GUIDE TO
PRACTICAL STITCHES

First Published in the UK in 2014 by
Apple Press
74-77 White Lion Street
London N1 9PF
UK

www.apple-press.com

10 9 8 7 6 5 4 3 2 1

ISBN: 978-1-84543-516-5

Manufactured in China

Commisioning Editor: Isheeta Mustafi
Editor: Cath Senker
Assistant Editor: Tamsin Richardson
Art Editor: Jennifer Osborne
Design and Cover: Lucy Smith
Layout: Anna Gyseman
Photography by: Sherry Heck
Styling: Heather Sansky
Illustrations: Robert Brandt

THE HOME SEWER'S GUIDE TO
PRACTICAL STITCHES

THE ULTIMATE GUIDE TO SEWING
SEAMS, HEMS, DARTS... AND MORE!

NICOLE VASBINDER

APPLE

Contents

Section 1

Machine Stitches

Section 2

Hand Stitches

Section 3

Tools and Equipment

How to use this book

I have been sewing for about 30 years and consider myself a fairly advanced seamstress. But like many sewers, most of my sewing uses just a few of the basic stitches on my sewing machine. I assumed all those 'other' stitches were decorative and my machine manual did not have much information on how to use them. As I researched, I discovered that each of the stitches has a specific purpose and makes certain sewing tasks easier and faster. Some of them replicate the look of hand stitching at the press of a button!

I also began to explore hand stitching. Learning couture techniques that cannot be accomplished on a machine and mastering hand techniques allowed me to sew on the go.

This book is a complete and illustrated guide to machine and hand stitches for the modern sewist and is designed to be an ideal worktop companion. What's the best stitch to hand-set a zipper? When should you use a diagonal tacking stitch? What are the various uses of a blind hem stitch? Whether sewing clothes from patterns, designing your own sewing projects, or executing simple repairs, this book is a comprehensive and ready reference consolidating all the most useful and practical information you need to choose and use every kind of sewing stitch.

Following a simple entry-based format, each stitch entry shows a photographed example of the stitch on fabric followed by illustrated tutorials of how to execute the stitch. Essential facts for each stitch are listed in an easy-to-read bullet list and cover everything from alternative names for that stitch, the best fabric types, common uses of a particular stitch, substitute stitches, and threads and needles that might be specific to that stitch. In addition, each entry has practical hints and tips to improve your sewing, as well as a symbol indicating the level of difficulty (see key below).

Section One covers 50 of the most useful machine stitches. Using these stitches is contingent on that stitch being available on your sewing machine. If it isn't, would you know what would make an appropriate replacement? This section explains the purpose of each stitch and offers suggestions for other stitches that can be used instead. Section Two is devoted to hand stitching and explores the stitches every sewist should know how to do as well as a few special tricks. Section Three covers mechanical, computerised and vintage sewing machines as well as the needles, threads and presser feet needed to accomplish all these stitches.

Whether you're just starting out with your first sewing machine or have been sewing for a while and want to build on your skills, this book gives you practical advice and tips to master techniques you didn't think you could do.

I sincerely hope that this book becomes an inspiring part of your sewing library and pushes you to a new level of creativity and confidence. Happy sewing!

Key

BASIC

INTERMEDIATE

ADVANCED

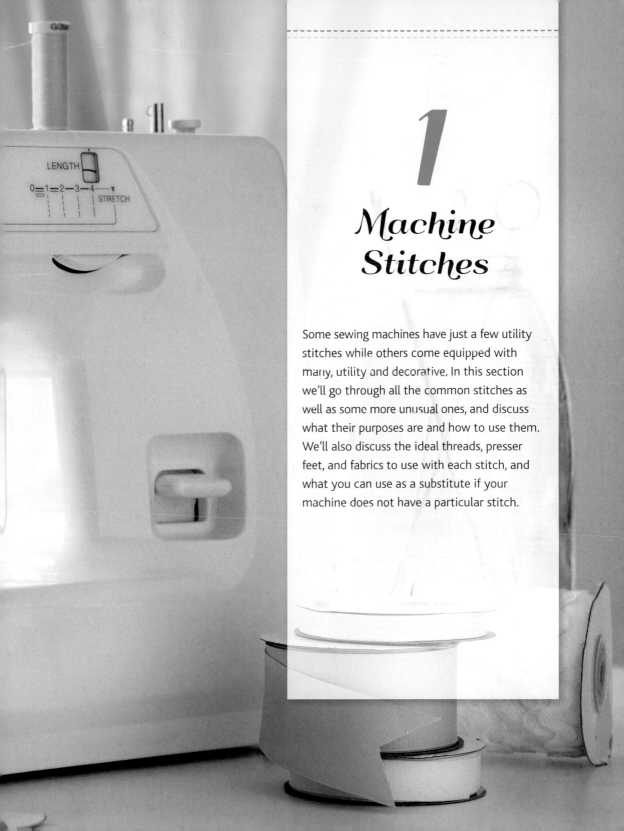

1

Machine Stitches

Some sewing machines have just a few utility stitches while others come equipped with many, utility and decorative. In this section we'll go through all the common stitches as well as some more unusual ones, and discuss what their purposes are and how to use them. We'll also discuss the ideal threads, presser feet, and fabrics to use with each stitch, and what you can use as a substitute if your machine does not have a particular stitch.

Straight Stitch

This is the most basic and frequently used stitch. It is available on all sewing machines and looks like a dashed line. It is the essential construction stitch used to connect two pieces of fabric and is used for sewing seams, darts and hems. It is also used for topstitching, tacking and installing zippers. The standard length for basic sewing is 2.5mm or 11 stitches per inch. Longer lengths are used for temporary tacking and shorter lengths for strong securing stitches. Straight stitches do not stretch so don't use them for stretch knits.

ESSENTIAL FACTS

Also known as
Basic stitch

Key feature
Looks like a dashed line

Substitute stitch
No substitute stitch

Common uses
Seams, hems, topstitching, darts, gathers, inserting zippers and tacking

Presser foot
All-purpose or straight stitch for seams, zipper for inserting zippers

Fabric type
All woven fabrics

Thread type
Polyester or cotton

Needle type
Universal, size appropriate for fabric

▶ SEE ALSO
All-purpose foot, page 158

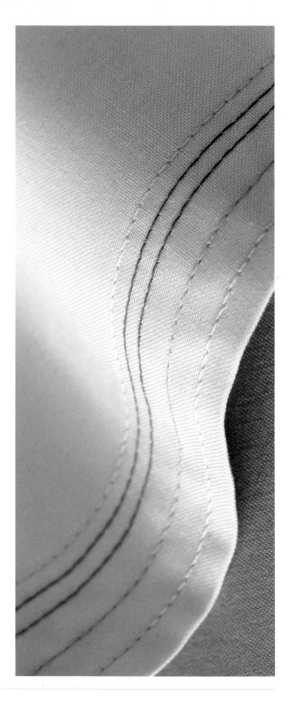

HOW TO SEW A BASIC SEAM USING STRAIGHT STITCH

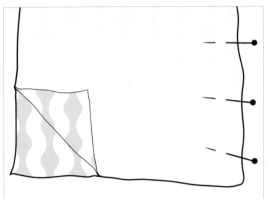

1 Lay the fabrics with the two right sides facing and line up the raw edges evenly. Pin the fabric edges together, inserting the pins perpendicular to the fabric edge.

2 Line up the fabric edges on the appropriate seam guide and 6mm (¼in) down from the top edge. Lower the presser foot. Set your machine to straight stitch and adjust the stitch length to 2.5mm.

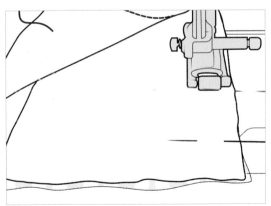

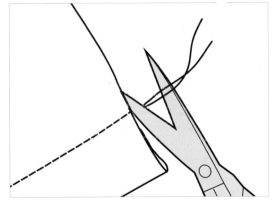

3 Backstitch to the edge and then stitch forward. Make sure to remove the pins before stitching over them.

4 Just before the end, make three to four backstitches and then stitch off the edge. Trim the thread tails at the beginning and end of the seam.

 EXPERT TIP What is the secret to perfectly straight seams? Don't watch the needle. If you are watching the needle, then you do not know where the fabric edges are and you will start to drift. Instead, keep your eyes and fabric edges on the seam guide.

HOW TO SEW A HEM USING STRAIGHT STITCH

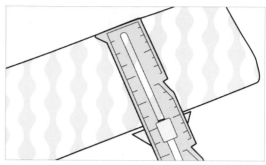

1 Press the hem to the wrong side of the fabric and to the full amount of the hem allowance. Use a seam gauge or tape measure to make sure it's accurate.

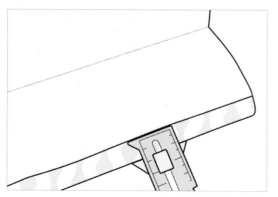

2 Unfold the hem, turn the raw edge of the fabric under 6mm (1/4in) and press again. Refold the hem before pinning it for sewing. Again, use a seam gauge or tape measure to make sure it's accurate.

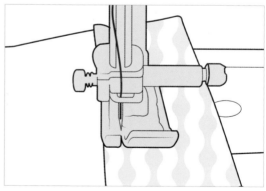

3 Set the machine to straight stitch and adjust the stitch length to 2.5mm. Work from the wrong side of the fabric. Line up the fold against the left edge of the presser foot and adjust needle to the left position. Topstitch in place.

▶ SEE ALSO
All-purpose foot, page 158

HOW TO SEW A DART USING STRAIGHT STITCH

1 Mark the dart, following the pattern markings, using tailor's chalk, fabric marker or tailor's tacks. Fold the dart so that the right sides are facing and pin to hold in place. Set your machine to straight stitch and adjust the stitch length to 2.5mm.

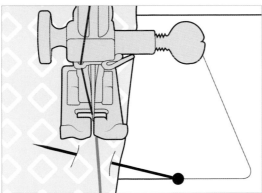

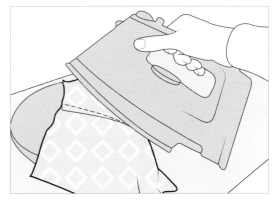

2 Sew the dart from the widest part towards the point. Backstitch at the wide part, but don't backstitch at the point. Instead, shorten the stitch length to 1mm when you are 6mm (¹/₄in) from the dart point. Make sure the last couple of stitches are right on the fold.

3 Press the dart to finish, using a tailor's ham to maintain the shape. Press vertical darts towards the centre of the garment and press horizontal darts down towards the bottom of the garment.

▶ SEE ALSO
Tailor's tack, page 134

 EXPERT TIP If you are using a thick fabric, you can slash darts down the centre after stitching and press them open to reduce bulk.

HOW TO INSTALL A ZIPPER USING STRAIGHT STITCH

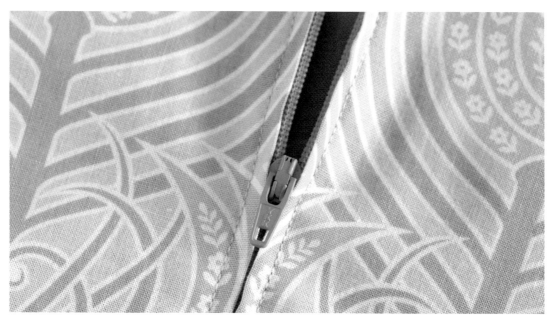

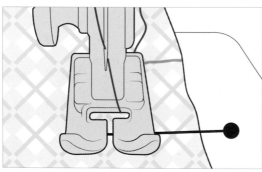

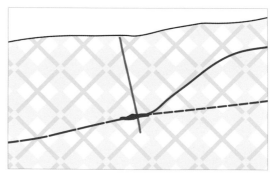

1 Pin the seam together with right sides facing. Mark where the zipper stop will go. Set your machine to straight stitch and adjust the stitch length to 2.5mm. Sew the seam together from the mark down to the bottom of the seam.

2 Adjust the stitch length to at least 4mm to tack the seam together from the top down to your mark, to join with the shorter stitches. Press the seam open.

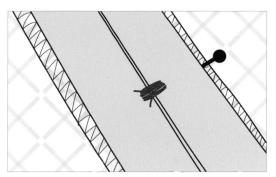

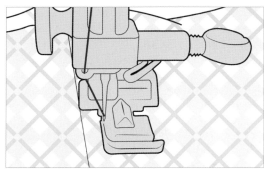

3 Working on the wrong side, place the zipper face down with the zipper coil centred on the seam. Align the zipper stop at your mark and pin the zipper in place.

4 Install the zipper foot so that the foot is attached on its left half. Set the stitch length back to 2.5mm. With the fabric right side up, align the left edge of the foot on the seam and stitch down the right side of the zipper. Just before the zipper stop, with the needle in the fabric, lift the presser foot to pivot the fabric and zipper to stitch across the bottom, then backstitch to finish.

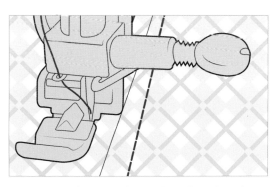

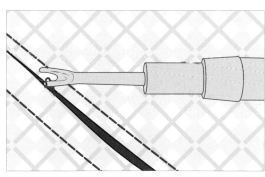

5 Now move the zipper foot to the right and stitch down the left side of the zipper to the bottom, finishing with backstitch.

6 With a seam ripper, carefully rip out the tacking stitches, then press the seam flat.

▶ SEE ALSO
Tacking stitch, page 16; zigzag stitch, page 18; overcasting stitch, page 46; zipper foot, page 160

 EXPERT TIP Finish the seam allowances by using a zigzag or overcast stitch before installing the zipper.

Tacking Stitch

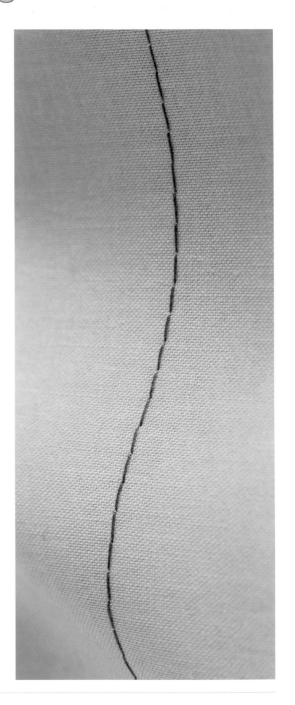

The tacking stitch is a very long straight stitch available on many computerised machines. It is designed to hold fabrics together temporarily. Because it is easy to unpick, it is used to sew seams together during fitting. You can try on a garment to check for fit and then simply pull out the stitches without damaging the fabric. This stitch can be used to hold slippery fabrics together before sewing the seams permanently and to hold zippers in place before final stitching. Make sure you use a needle type and size suitable for your fabric. Use silk or all-purpose thread.

ESSENTIAL FACTS

Also known as
Temporary stitch

Key feature
An extra-long straight stitch

Substitute stitch
Straight stitch, with a length of at least 4mm, or hand tacking

Common uses
Temporary stitches for fitting, inserting zippers and holding slippery fabrics

Presser foot
All-purpose

Fabric type
All, appropriate for project

Thread type
Polyester, cotton or silk

Needle type
Universal, size appropriate for fabric

▶ SEE ALSO
Hand tacking, page 114

HOW TO TACK A SEAM USING TACKING STITCH

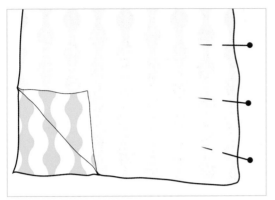

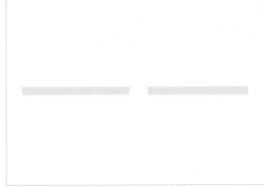

1 Lay the fabrics with the two right sides facing and line up the raw edges evenly. Pin the fabric edges together with the pins perpendicular to the fabric edge.

2 Line up the fabric edges on the appropriate seam guide. Lower the presser foot and select tacking stitch on your machine.

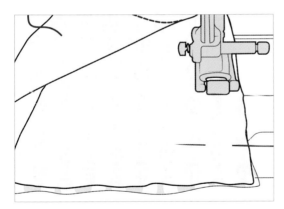

3 Leaving long thread tails to make it easier to pull the stitches out, stitch at the end of the seam and work forwards. The feed dogs will move the fabric very quickly so don't press the foot pedal too hard. Make sure you remove the pins before stitching over them.

 EXPERT TIP Using a thread that contrasts with the fabric makes the tacking stitches more visible, which allows for easier removal.

Zigzag Stitch

The zigzag stitch is found on all sewing machines except straight-stitch-only machines. It is used to overcast seam allowances and prevent fraying on woven fabric edges, and to sew stretch knits. It can be used as a decorative topstitch and to sew on appliqués. Adjust the stitch length and width to create different stitches. For basic sewing use a stitch that is 2.5mm long and 3.5mm wide; for satin stitching appliqués and embroidery use a 0.5mm long/4–5mm wide stitch; for stretch sewing use a 2.5mm long/0.5mm wide stitch.

ESSENTIAL FACTS

Also known as
Not known by other names

Key feature
Stitches swing left and right

Substitute stitch
Satin stitch, stem stitch or overcast stitch

Common uses
Finishing seams, stretch sewing, appliqué and topstitching

Presser foot
All-purpose, satin stitch or overcast

Fabric type
All, appropriate for project

Thread type
Polyester for overcasting, sewing knits, topstitching, and appliqués; decorative for topstitching and appliqués

Needle type
Universal for woven fabrics; stretch or ballpoint for knits

▶ SEE ALSO
Overcast foot, page 162

HOW TO FINISH A SEAM USING A ZIGZAG STITCH

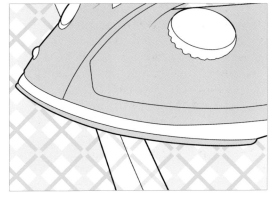

1 Install the all-purpose foot. Select a straight stitch with a stitch length of 2.5mm. With fabric right sides facing and raw edges aligned, stitch a basic straight seam; backstitch at the beginning and end. Trim the thread tails.

2 Press the seam open.

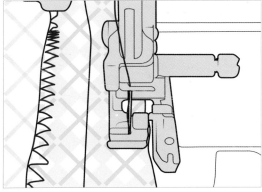

3 Install the overcast foot and set it to a zigzag stitch with a stitch length of 2.5mm and a width of 4mm. Align the raw edge along the blade and lower the presser foot. Stitch the edge. The needle should go just off the edge of the fabric.

4 Repeat for the other seam allowance. Trim the thread tails at the end.

 EXPERT TIP 'Walk' the needle a couple of stitches, by turning the hand wheel, to make sure it clears the pin on the overcast foot.

HOW TO SEW KNITS WITH ZIGZAG STITCH

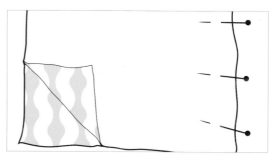

1 Attach the all-purpose foot to the sewing machine and insert a stretch or ballpoint needle. Set your machine to a zigzag stitch that is 2.5mm long and 1mm wide. Lay your fabric with the right sides facing and line up the raw edges evenly. Pin the fabric edges together with the pins perpendicular to the fabric edge.

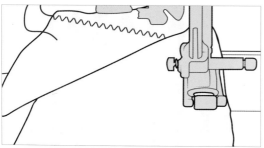

2 Line up the fabric edges on the appropriate seam guide. Lower the presser foot. Stitch the seam, making sure you backstitch at the beginning and the end.

3 Press the seams open.

 EXPERT TIP You may need to adjust to a slightly wider zigzag stitch for particularly stretchy knits, such as swimsuit fabrics. The wider the zigzag, the more stretch it has. However, if it is too wide, the stitches will show when the seam is pressed open. Always do a test stitch on a spare swatch of the fabric.

▶ SEE ALSO
Stretch needles, page 151

HOW TO APPLIQUÉ USING ZIGZAG STITCH

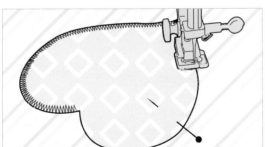

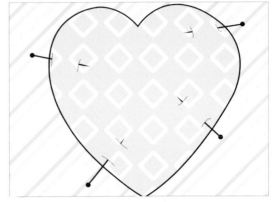

1 Place the appliqué face up on the fabric it will be stitched to and pin it in place with the pins perpendicular to the fabric edge.

2 Set your machine to a zigzag stitch that is 0.5mm long and 4mm wide. Install the satin stitch foot on your machine. Line up the edge of the appliqué in the centre split of the presser foot. This will be your seam guide. Stitch around the appliqué, making sure you leave long thread tails at the beginning and end instead of backstitching.

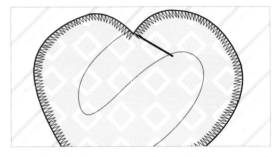

3 Working by hand, use a needle to pull the top thread tails through to the wrong side of the fabric, then tie them off.

▶ SEE ALSO
Satin stitch foot, page 158

Three-step Zigzag Stitch

The three-step zigzag stitch differs from a standard zigzag stitch in having three small stitches in each direction rather than one long stitch. It has all the stretch of a zigzag stitch but because the stitches are shorter, they don't snag as easily as a standard zigzag, even at the widest setting. This stitch is available on most sewing machines and is designed for attaching elastics to waistbands, legholes, armholes and necklines; and for hemming knits. It can also be used to repair tears in woven and knit fabrics.

ESSENTIAL FACTS

Also known as
Multistep zigzag stitch, elastic stitch and tricot stitch

Key feature
A zigzag made of three small stitches in each direction

Substitute stitch
Zigzag stitch

Common uses
Attaching elastic and mending

Presser foot
All-purpose

Fabric type
All, appropriate for project

Thread type
Polyester for knits and elastic; polyester or cotton for mending

Needle type
Match needle type to fabric

▶ SEE ALSO
Serpentine stitch, page 64;
All-purpose foot, page 158

HOW TO MEND TEARS USING THREE-STEP ZIGZAG STITCH

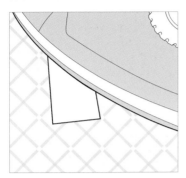 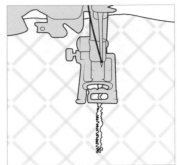 

1 Trim any frayed edges and back the tear in the fabric by ironing a strip of fusible interfacing to the wrong side of the fabric, pulling together the torn edges.

2 Select the three-step zigzag stitch. Centre the tear under the presser foot. Adjust the stitch length to 1mm and the width to a setting that will span the torn edges of the fabric.

3 Then stitch over the torn edges, catching each edge with the bite of the zigzag stitch. If the first pass doesn't fully cover it, stitch over the tear a second time.

HOW TO APPLY ELASTIC USING THREE-STEP ZIGZAG STITCH

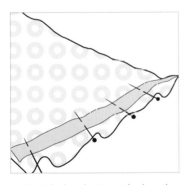  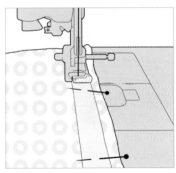

1 Stretch the elastic to the length of the seam and pin it in place every 5cm (2in) or so. Make sure that the elastic is evenly stretched.

2 Insert a stretch or ballpoint needle in the machine and select a three-step zigzag stitch 2.5mm long and as wide as the elastic. Centre the elastic under the presser foot.

3 Backstitch at the start and then stitch over the elastic, stretching it flat between pins. Backstitch at the end.

 EXPERT TIP Braided elastics get narrower as they stretch and should never be stitched through or they may unravel. They should be used inside casings. Knitted elastics don't become narrower when stretched and can be stitched onto fabric.

Stem Stitch

The stem stitch looks like a lightning bolt. It is a very narrow zigzag for which the needle takes a stitch back and then forwards and is designed for seaming stretch-knit fabrics on a standard sewing machine. It can be used for decorative topstitching as well. Stem stitch has much more stretch than a narrow zigzag and the seams can be pressed open without the stitches showing. Stem stitch is available on most computerised machines and some mechanical machines.

ESSENTIAL FACTS

Also known as
Stretch stitch

Key feature
Looks like a lightning bolt

Substitute stitch
Zigzag stitch or triple straight stitch

Common uses
Seams on knits and topstitching

Presser foot
All-purpose or walking, which can help prevent knit fabrics from stretching and rippling

Fabric type
Stretch knits

Thread type
Polyester

Needle type
Stretch or ballpoint; note that a universal needle can damage knit fabrics

▶ SEE ALSO
Walking foot, page 159

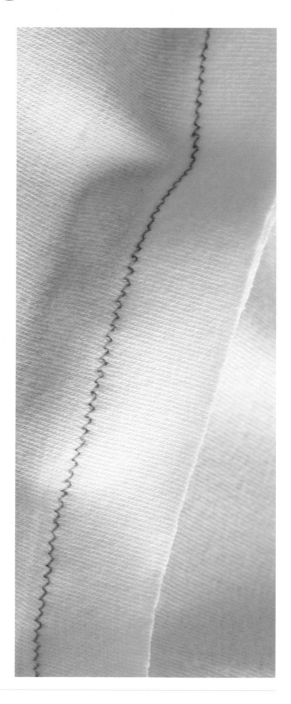

HOW TO SEW KNITS USING STEM STITCH

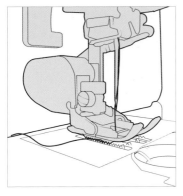

1 Install the walking foot and insert a stretch needle.

2 Select stem stitch with a length of 2.5mm and a width of 1mm.

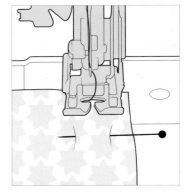

3 Pin the edges of the fabric together with the right sides facing. Line up the fabric edges on the appropriate seam guide and 6mm (¼in) down from the top edge. Lower the presser foot, backstitch, then stitch forwards. Remove the pins before stitching over them.

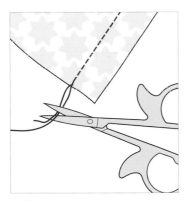

4 Trim the thread tails at the beginning and end of the seam.

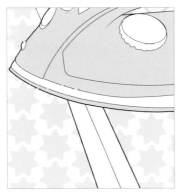

5 Press the seam open.

 EXPERT TIP If the fabric doesn't feed, lengthen the stitch to 3mm.

Triple Straight Stitch

In triple straight stitch, the machine takes one stitch forward, one back, and one forward again. This makes a very strong seam, ideal for high-stress seams such as the crotch on a pair of trousers. Since the feed dogs move the fabric back and forth, this stitch has stretch and is perfect for seaming knits. It is excellent for topstitching in a contrasting colour as the stitches are heavier than a basic straight stitch. This stitch is available on nearly all sewing machines. On mechanical machines, select a standard straight stitch and adjust the stitch length to SS (stretch stitch).

ESSENTIAL FACTS

Also known as
Stretch straight stitch and treble stitch

Key feature
Three straight stitches on top of each other

Substitute stitch
Stem stitch

Common uses
Stretch seams on knits and reinforcing stitches on high-stress seams

Presser foot
All-purpose for woven fabrics, walking for knit fabrics to help prevent stretching and rippling

Fabric type
Knits and woven fabrics

Thread type
Polyester for knits; polyester, cotton or decorative for topstitching

Needle type
Universal for wovens; stretch for knits

▶ SEE ALSO
Tacking stitch, page 16;
Walking foot, page 159

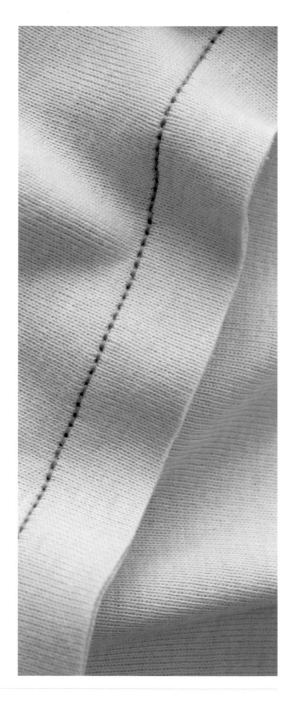

HOW TO SEW KNITS USING TRIPLE STRAIGHT STITCH

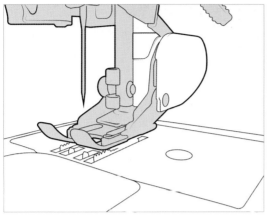

1 Install the walking foot and insert a stretch needle.

2 Select triple straight stitch with a length of 2.5mm.

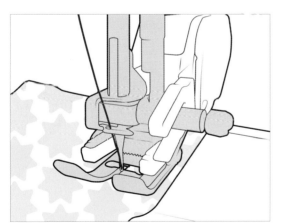

3 Pin the fabric edges together with right sides facing. Line up the fabric edges on the seam guide at the top edge. Lower the presser foot. Don't backstitch, just stitch forwards. Make sure you remove the pins before stitching over them. At the end, stitch off the edge.

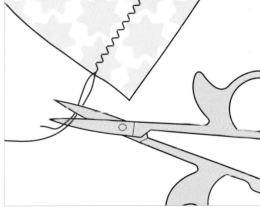

4 Trim the thread tails at the beginning and end of the seam. Press the seam open.

 EXPERT TIP This stitch is very difficult to remove as each stitch is backstitched. Always tack seams to ensure a proper fit before using the triple straight stitch for final construction seaming.

Ric Rac Stitch

The ric rac stitch is a zigzag stitch. The machine takes one stitch forward, one back, then one stitch forward. This heavy-duty stitch works wonderfully as bold topstitching in a contrasting colour. Because it can stretch, it can be used on woven fabrics and knits. It is available on most sewing machines. On mechanical machines, select a standard zigzag stitch and adjust the stitch length to SS (stretch stitch). If using a computerised sewing machine, just push a button to select the stitch. On some machines it is the same as the triple straight stitch and you need to adjust to a wider width to switch to ric rac.

ESSENTIAL FACTS

Also known as
Triple zigzag stitch

Key feature
Three zigzag stitches on top of each other

Substitute stitch
Zigzag stitch or triple straight stitch

Common uses
Topstitching

Presser foot
All-purpose or satin stitch, on which the deeper indentation on the bottom allows for the build-up of stitches

Fabric type
Knits and woven fabrics

Thread type
Polyester, cotton or a decorative variegated or metallic

Needle type
Universal, size appropriate for fabric

▶ SEE ALSO
Satin stitch foot, page 158

HOW TO TOPSTITCH USING RIC RAC STITCH

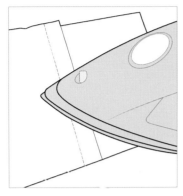

1 Using a basic straight stitch, sew seams in the usual manner and then press the seams to one side.

2 Install the satin stitch foot, thread your machine with the desired thread, and select the ric rac stitch set to the length and width you require.

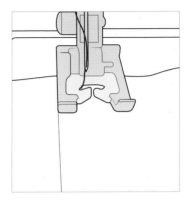

3 Position the fabric face up under the presser foot so that the seam edge is against the edge of the presser foot. Make sure the seam allowances are under the foot so that you are stitching through all three layers. Lower the presser foot.

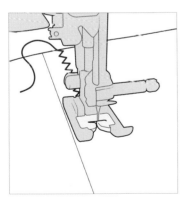

4 Don't backstitch; instead, leave long thread tails at the beginning and end.

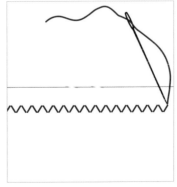

5 Working by hand, use a needle to pull the top thread tails through to the wrong side of the fabric, then tie them off.

 EXPERT TIP Topstitching is a good way to hold a seam allowance in place and keep edges flat. It can also be purely decorative. You can also press your seams open and then topstitch down either side of the seam.

Straight Blind Hem Stitch

The straight blind hem stitch is made up of several straight stitches and a large zigzag to the left. It is used for hemming woven fabrics and is practically invisible from the right side where you will see only a tiny stitch every 13mm (½in) or so. On the wrong side of the hem you will see the series of straight stitches and the big zigzag. It works best on straighter edges; extreme curves are difficult with this stitch. The straight blind hem stitch is available on most sewing machines.

ESSENTIAL FACTS

Also known as
Invisible hem

Key feature
Several straight stitches with one big zigzag to the left

Substitute stitch
Stretch blind hem stitch

Common uses
Hems

Presser foot
Blind hem

Fabric type
Woven fabrics

Thread type
Polyester in a colour that is a perfect match for the fabric or invisible thread for multicoloured fabrics

Needle type
Universal for medium-weight fabrics; Microtex for fine fabrics

▶ SEE ALSO
Stretch blind hem stitch, page 32;
Blind hem foot, page 162

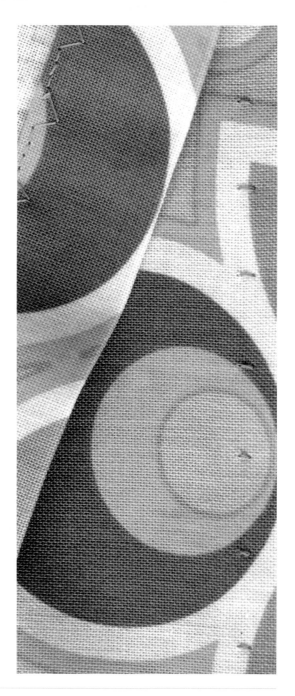

HOW TO STITCH A HEM USING STRAIGHT BLIND HEM STITCH

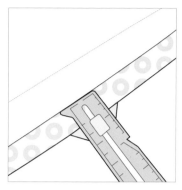

1 Press the hem to the wrong side of the fabric, to the full amount of the hem allowance. Unfold and press the raw edge under 10mm (³/₈in).

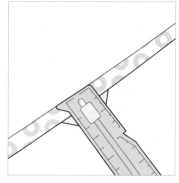

2 Now fold the hem back so that 6mm (¹/₄in) of the folded edge extends out.

3 Install the blind hem foot on your machine and select the straight blind hem stitch with a stitch length of 2.5mm.

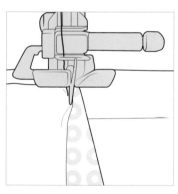

4 Using the hand wheel, walk your machine until the needle swings to the far left zigzag. The needle should just barely catch the fold. The fold should butt up against the bar; use this as your seam guide.

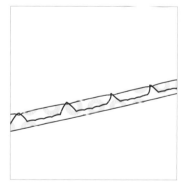

5 Start stitching. The big zigzag will catch just a thread of the fold, and the straight stitches will stitch the folded edge in place.

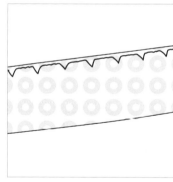

6 Unfold the hem and press it flat.

 EXPERT TIP If you see a big stitch on the right side, you stitched too far onto the fold. If it doesn't catch, you stitched too far from the fold.

Stretch Blind Hem Stitch

The stretch blind hem stitch consists of several small zigzag stitches with one large zigzag to the left. Consisting entirely of zigzags it can stretch, making it perfect for hemming knits. The stretch blind hem stitch can also be used for hemming woven fabrics as the small zigzags will overcast the raw edge and prevent the fabric edge from ravelling. This is one of the basic utility stitches and is available on almost all sewing machines. Like the straight blind hem stitch, it is practically invisible from the right side. On the wrong side of the hem you will see the zigzag stitches. It is most successful on straight edges.

ESSENTIAL FACTS

Also known as
Invisible hem

Key feature
Several small zigzags with one big zigzag to the left

Substitute stitch
Long wide zigzag stitch

Common uses
Hems

Presser foot
Blind hem

Fabric type
Knits and woven fabrics

Thread type
Polyester in a colour that is a perfect match for the fabric, or invisible thread for multicoloured fabrics

Needle type
Universal for woven fabrics; stretch or ballpoint for knits

▶ SEE ALSO
Blind hem foot, page 162

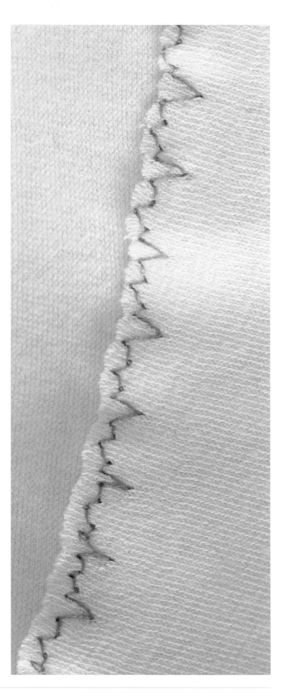

HOW TO STITCH A HEM USING STRETCH BLIND HEM STITCH

1 Press the hem to the wrong side of the fabric, to the full amount of the hem allowance. Use an adjustable seam guide or tape measure for accuracy.

2 Now fold the hem back so that 6mm (1/4in) of the raw edge extends out.

3 Install the blind hem foot on your machine and select the stretch blind hem stitch with a stitch length of 2.5mm.

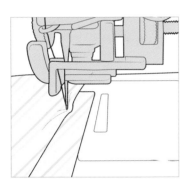

4 Using the hand wheel, walk your machine until the needle swings to the far left zigzag. The needle should just barely catch the fold. Using the hand screw, adjust the bar on the foot so that it comes right up against the fold. Use this as your seam guide.

5 Start stitching. The big zigzag will catch just a thread of the fold, and the small zigzag stitches will overcast the raw edge.

6 Unfold the hem and press it flat.

 EXPERT TIP Some jersey knits are notorious for curling along the edges. Spraying starch on the fabric edge before sewing can hold the edge stiff and make it easier to hem.

Manual Buttonhole

A basic buttonhole is a rectangle consisting of zigzag stitches. The long sides (beads), are made with a very narrow and short zigzag; the ends (bartacks), are made with a wide zigzag and 0mm stitch length. The manual buttonhole is found on most machines. Each of the four sides is made with a separate stitch on the pattern selection dial. The length and width will automatically adjust as you go through the sequence. You can make a standard box buttonhole with a manual buttonhole stitch in any length you like.

ESSENTIAL FACTS

Also known as
Four-step buttonhole

Key feature
A basic buttonhole with each side a separate stitch

Substitute stitch
No substitute stitch

Common uses
Standard buttonholes on garments, accessories and home décor projects

Presser foot
Manual buttonhole for buttonholes of any length; sliding manual buttonhole for buttonholes of up to 28mm (1¹/₈in) in length

Fabric type
All, appropriate for project

Thread type
Polyester in a matching or contrasting colour, or novelty thread for buttonholes that are a design element

Needle type
Universal, size appropriate for fabric

▶ SEE ALSO
Manual buttonhole foot, page 161

HOW TO STITCH A MANUAL BUTTONHOLE

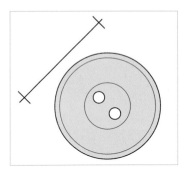

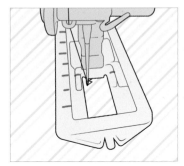

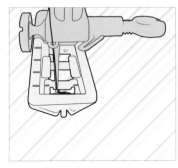

1 Position the buttonhole on the fabric and then mark it with chalk or a fabric marker. Install the buttonhole foot on your sewing machine and adjust the slider so that your marking is perfectly framed in the window. Lower the presser foot.

2 Adjust the stitch selector on the machine to buttonhole step 1 and stitch length to 0.5mm. Stitch down the left side of the buttonhole. Ensure the last stitch is on the left side of the zigzag and the needle is out of the fabric.

3 Adjust the selector to buttonhole step 2 and work five stitches so that you finish on the right side. The stitch will now automatically adjust to a wider, shorter zigzag. Make sure the needle is out of the fabric when you finish the last stitch.

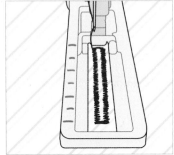

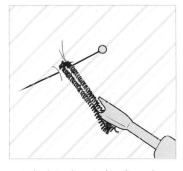

4 Adjust the selector to buttonhole step 3 and stitch back up to the top. The stitch will be the same as step 1 but you'll be working in reverse. As you sew, the window will slide back open. Make sure the last stitch is on the right and the needle is out of the fabric.

5 Adjust the selector to step 4 (often the same as step 2) and work five stitches. Make sure the needle is out of the fabric when you finish the last stitch.

6 To lock in the stitch, adjust the selector to straight stitch, change the stitch length to 0mm, and work three to four stitches. Trim off the threads and cut open the buttonhole, using either a seam ripper or scissors.

 EXPERT TIP Buttonholes don't just have to be used with buttons; try using them as drawstring openings.

Automatic Buttonhole

Automatic buttonholes are perfect for projects with many buttons. The process is fast and they will all come out identical. Use the automatic buttonhole foot and insert the button into the extension on the back. The machine will then size the buttonhole to fit that button. Automatic buttonholes are found on computerised and some mechanical sewing machines. Each side of the buttonhole is created with the same stitch on the pattern selection dial. The length and width will adjust for each side of the buttonhole. Automatic buttonholes can be a variety of shapes.

ESSENTIAL FACTS

Also known as
One-step buttonhole

Key feature
A basic buttonhole with each side the same stitch

Substitute stitch
No substitute stitch

Common uses
Standard buttonholes on garments, accessories and home décor projects

Presser foot
Automatic buttonhole

Fabric type
All, appropriate for project

Thread type
Polyester in a matching or contrasting colour, or novelty thread for buttonholes that are a design element

Needle type
Universal, size appropriate for fabric

▶ SEE ALSO
Buttonhole foot, page 161

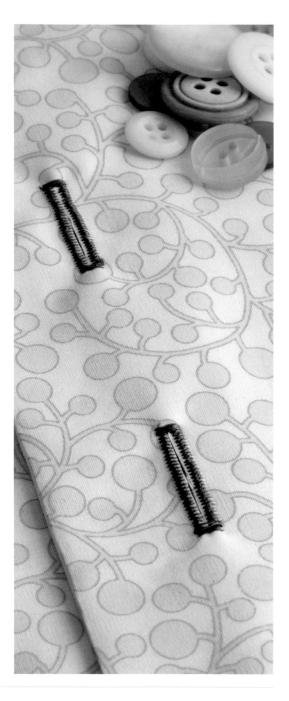

HOW TO STITCH AN AUTOMATIC BUTTONHOLE

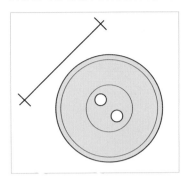

1 Mark the starting point for the buttonhole on the fabric with chalk or a fabric marker.

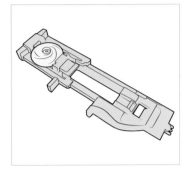

2 Insert the button into the slot on the back of the buttonhole foot. The window will automatically adjust to the correct size for that button. Install the foot on your machine.

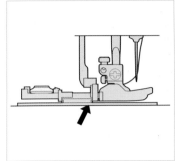

3 Lower the buttonhole lever so that it sits between the two tabs on the left side of the foot.

4 Adjust the pattern selector to buttonhole stitch.

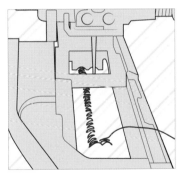

5 Position the foot so that you are starting at the beginning (see tip below). Lower the presser and start stitching. The machine will first stitch one bead and across the bottom – one bartack – then the other bead and bartack.

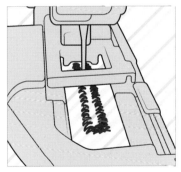

6 To finish, the machine will work a couple of lock stitches to help secure the buttonhole, and may even beep to tell you when it is done. Trim off the threads and cut open the buttonhole, using either a seam ripper or scissors.

 EXPERT TIP Some machines will start stitching at the top of the buttonhole and then work their way around anticlockwise. Other machines start at the bottom and work their way around clockwise. Always do a practice buttonhole to be sure.

Rounded Buttonhole

The rounded buttonhole is horizontal. The rounded end prevents fabric strain and should be near the centre line of the garment. Rounded buttonholes are usually only available on computerised sewing machines. Some machines offer more than one type, including narrow rounded buttonholes for lightweight fabrics and wide rounded buttonholes for heavier fabrics.

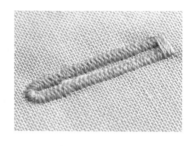

HOW TO STITCH A ROUNDED BUTTONHOLE

1 Mark the starting point for the buttonhole on the fabric with chalk or a fabric marker.

2 Insert button in the guide plate on the automatic buttonhole foot. Attach foot. Lower buttonhole lever so it is between the brackets.

3 Now select the rounded buttonhole stitch.

4 Position the foot to start at the beginning (see tip p. 39). After sewing the buttonhole itself, the machine will sew reinforcement stitches. Lift the presser foot.

5 Remove the fabric, trim threads and cut open the buttonhole, using a seam ripper or scissors.

ESSENTIAL FACTS

Also known as
Horizontal buttonhole

Key feature
A buttonhole with one end rounded

Substitute stitch
Standard buttonhole stitch

Common uses
On garments, for blouses, waistbands, shirts, dresses and jackets

Presser foot
Automatic buttonhole

Fabric type
Light- to medium-weight fabrics

Thread type
Cotton or polyester

Needle type
Universal, size appropriate for fabric

▶ SEE ALSO
Buttonhole foot, page 161

Keyhole Buttonhole

The keyhole buttonhole is designed for shank buttons; the rounded end opens wider than on standard buttonholes. The keyhole should be positioned so that the button sits in the keyhole when fastened. Keyhole buttonholes are usually only available on computerised machines. There may be a variety of styles for different weights of fabric, along with novelty styles to add a decorative detail.

HOW TO STITCH A KEYHOLE BUTTONHOLE

1 Mark the starting point for the buttonhole on the fabric with chalk or a fabric marker.

2 Insert the button into the slot on buttonhole foot. The window slides to correct size. Install buttonhole foot. Lower the buttonhole lever between tabs on side of foot.

3 Now select the keyhole buttonhole stitch. Position the foot to start at the beginning (see tip below).

4 The machine will stitch half the rounded end, up one side, across the top, back down the other side, and the other rounded half all in one step. Trim off the threads.

ESSENTIAL FACTS

Also known as
Not known by other names

Key feature
A buttonhole with one end having a round keyhole shape

Substitute stitch
Standard buttonhole

Common uses
Garments with shank buttons

Presser foot
Automatic buttonhole

Fabric type
Medium- to heavyweight fabrics

Thread type
Cotton or polyester

Needle type
Universal, size appropriate for fabric

▶ SEE ALSO
Buttonhole foot, page 161

EXPERT TIP Always do a practice buttonhole on a scrap of the fabric you will be using. You may need a longer stitch length for fabrics that don't feed easily, such as flannel.

Stretch Buttonhole

The stretch buttonhole uses enlarged zigzag stitches on the beads. These longer zigzags allow knit fabrics to stretch so that the fabric doesn't distort. A stretch buttonhole can also be used on woven fabrics to give a hand-stitched, heirloom buttonhole look. Stretch buttonholes are only available on computerised sewing machines. You can adjust the stitch length and width for different looks and degrees of stretch.

HOW TO STITCH A STRETCH BUTTONHOLE

1 Mark the starting point for the buttonhole on the fabric with chalk or a fabric marker. Insert the button into the slot on the buttonhole foot. The window will slide to the correct size. Install the buttonhole foot and lower the buttonhole lever between the tabs on the side of the foot.

2 Select the stretch buttonhole.

3 Position the foot to start at the beginning (see tip p. 37). The machine will zigzag up one side, stitch across the top bartack, straight stitch back down to the bottom, stitch across the bottom bartack, and zigzag back up to the top. It will work a couple of lock stitches to make sure the buttonhole is secure.

4 Trim threads. Cut the buttonhole with a seam ripper or scissors.

see tip p. 37

ESSENTIAL FACTS

Also known as
Knit buttonhole and heirloom buttonhole

Key feature
A buttonhole on which the bead is an enlarged zigzag stitch

Substitute stitch
Standard buttonhole

Common uses
On knits or to give a hand-stitched look

Presser foot
Automatic buttonhole

Fabric type
Knits and woven fabrics

Thread type
Polyester, to match fabric

Needle type
Stretch for knits; universal for wovens

▶ SEE ALSO
Buttonhole foot, page 161

Eyelet Stitch

The eyelet stitch is a ring formed by radiating stitches. You can use eyelet stitches on belts in place of metal eyelets. Stitched eyelets are also perfect for anything that needs lacing, such as corsets. The stitch is available on some computerised sewing machines and you can usually choose from several sizes.

HOW TO STITCH AN EYELET

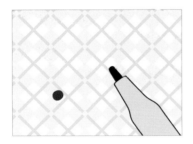

1 Mark the position of the eyelet with chalk or a fabric marker.

2 Attach the satin stitch foot to the sewing machine and select the eyelet stitch in the desired size.

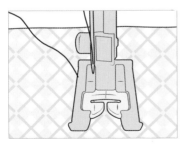

3 Position the fabric under the presser foot so that the mark is centred in the opening. Lower the presser foot. Start stitching. The machine will do several reinforcement stitches at the end to secure the thread.

4 Cut open the eyelet using an eyelet punch.

ESSENTIAL FACTS

Also known as
Ring stitch

Key feature
Stitches form a ring

Substitute stitch
Standard buttonhole, to make a small square buttonhole

Common uses
Secured openings for lacing or belts

Presser foot
Satin stitch, as the deep indentation on the bottom of the foot allows for the dense stitching

Fabric type
All, appropriate for project

Thread type
Polyester or decorative

Needle type
Universal, size appropriate for fabric

▶ SEE ALSO
Satin stitch foot, page 158

Bound Buttonhole

Bound buttonholes have the raw edges encased with facing pieces of fabric rather than stitches. The binding pieces of fabric are called lips. Use the same fabric as the garment for the lips or a contrast fabric to add a decorative element. Bound buttonholes can add a couture touch and are perfect for fabrics that might fray or tear with the many needle perforations of a stitched buttonhole. They are available on some computerised sewing machines.

HOW TO STITCH A BOUND BUTTONHOLE

1 Insert the button into the slot on the back of the buttonhole foot. The window will slide to the correct size. Then install the buttonhole foot and lower the buttonhole lever between the two tabs on the side of the foot.

2 Now select the bound buttonhole stitch.

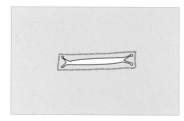

3 Cut out a rectangle of fabric that is about 25mm (1in) larger than the buttonhole. Pin it to the garment, right sides facing, and centred on top of the buttonhole. Mark the buttonhole position on the facing fabric with chalk or fabric marker.

4 Next cut down the centre of the buttonhole, starting and stopping 3mm (1/8in) from either end. Cut diagonally into each corner, but be careful not to cut through the stitches.

ESSENTIAL FACTS

Also known as
Welt buttonhole

Key feature
Buttonhole with straight stitches on each side

Substitute stitch
Straight stitch

Common uses
Buttonholes on fabrics that tend to fray

Presser foot
Automatic buttonhole

Fabric type
All, appropriate for project

Thread type
Polyester

Needle type
Universal, size appropriate for fabric

▶ SEE ALSO
Buttonhole foot, page 161

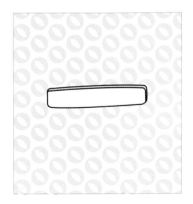

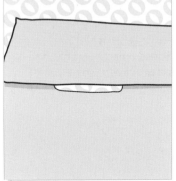

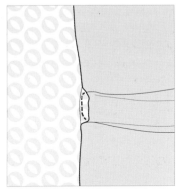

5 Pull the facing fabric through the opening you have just cut and press. You will have a clean finished window.

6 Work from the back. Fold the top part of the facing down to the centre of the window and press. This forms the top lip. Fold the bottom up to meet at the centre and press.

7 Switch to a zipper foot and understitch the corners to the seam allowance of the facing.

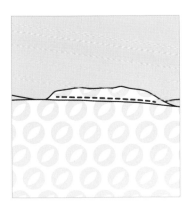

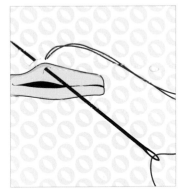

8 Understitch the long straight edges of the seam allowance to the facing. Trim away the excess facing fabric, leaving 6mm (1/4in) all around.

9 Repeat steps 3, 4 and 5 for the lining and the facing, and hand stitch the lining window to the bound buttonhole to make secure.

 EXPERT TIP If your machine does not have the bound buttonhole setting, just use a basic straight stitch with a length of 2mm (1/16in) and an all-purpose presser foot.

Button Stitch

The button stitch is designed to machine-stitch sew-through buttons. It is basically a wide zigzag stitch with a stitch length of 0mm. Button stitch is only available on some computerised sewing machines. So, if your machine does not have a button stitch setting, then you can simply use the zigzag stitch, adjust the stitch length to 0mm— or lower the feed dogs—and then adjust the stitch width to the distance between the holes in the button.

ESSENTIAL FACTS

Also known as
Not known by other names

Key feature
Wide zigzag with a stitch length of 0mm

Substitute stitch
Zigzag stitch

Common uses
Stitching on sew-through buttons

Presser foot
Button, as the short toes allow easy button positioning and the rubber coating on the toes holds the button securely during stitching

Fabric type
All, appropriate for project

Thread type
Polyester, topstitch or decorative

Needle type
Universal, size appropriate for fabric

▶ SEE ALSO
Button foot, page 161

HOW TO STITCH ON A BUTTON USING BUTTON STITCH

1 Install the button foot on your machine and select the button stitch.

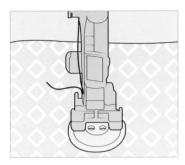

2 Position the button on the fabric, aligned with the presser foot, and lower the presser foot so that the holes on the button are between the toes on the button foot.

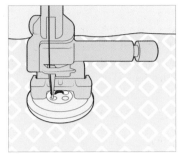

3 Using the hand wheel, walk the needle into one hole, then back up and down into the other hole. You may need to slightly adjust the stitch width to ensure that the needle goes cleanly through the holes. Once you are sure, then you can use the foot pedal to zigzag back and forth five or six times.

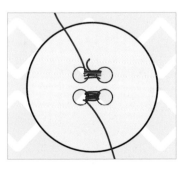

4 If you have a four-hole button, lift the presser foot to slide forward to the second set of holes.

5 Leave long thread tails when you are done stitching. Working by hand, thread these through a needle and pull them through to the wrong side of the fabric, then tie off and cut.

 EXPERT TIP This stitch cannot be used on shank buttons as the shank will make it impossible to position and stitch with a sewing machine. Shank buttons must be stitched on by hand.

Overcasting Stitch

The overcasting stitch has several straight stitches and then a big zigzag to the right. It is designed for finishing the raw edges of woven fabrics to prevent fraying and ravelling. The overcasting stitch is available on most mechanical machines and also on computerised sewing machines.

ESSENTIAL FACTS

Also known as
Overedge stitch

Key feature
Several straight stitches with a big zigzag to the right

Substitute stitch
Slant pin stitch and zigzag stitch

Common uses
Finishing raw edges on woven fabrics

Presser foot
Overcast, as the pin in it folds fabric edges flat, which prevents them from distorting during stitching

Fabric type
Woven fabrics

Thread type
Polyester

Needle type
Universal, size appropriate for fabric

▶ SEE ALSO
Zigzag stitch, page 18;
Overcast foot, page 162

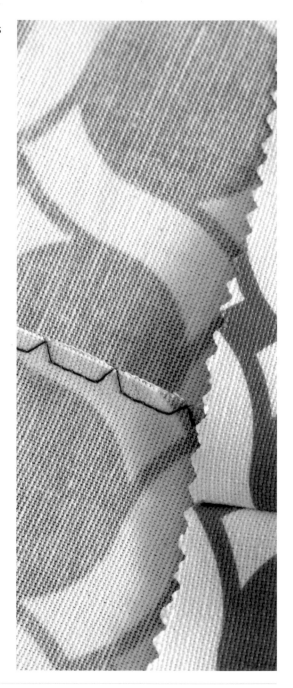

HOW TO OVERCAST A SEAM USING OVERCASTING STITCH

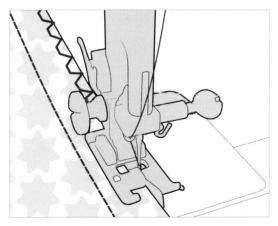

1 Sew the seam as usual and press it to one side. Attach the overcast foot to your sewing machine and select the overcast stitch.

2 Position the fabric under the presser foot so that the right edge of the fabric is butting up against the guide on the foot. Lower the presser foot.

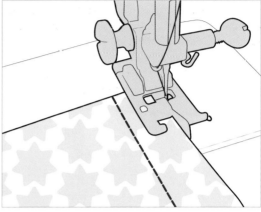

3 Using the guide on the foot as your seam guide, overcast the edge, making sure you backstitch at the beginning and end.

4 The needle should go just off the edge of the fabric on the right side.

 EXPERT TIP Always stitch the seams first and then finish them with overcasting stitches. If you overcast first, the fabric edges can roll slightly and this will change the seam allowances.

Stretch Overedge Stitch

The stretch overedge stitch mimics a serger stitch and is designed for sewing stretch-knit fabrics on a standard sewing machine. There is no need for a separate machine. It stitches and finishes a seam in one step. It has a straight stitch on the left side for seaming and zigzags on the right to overcast the edge. This seam is narrow and you need to make sure your seam allowances are 6mm (¼in) before sewing. The stretch overedge stitch is available on many mechanical machines and also on computerised sewing machines.

ESSENTIAL FACTS

Also known as
Serger stitch, overcast stitch and overlock stitch

Key feature
A straight stitch and an overcast stitch combined

Substitute stitch
Slant pin stitch

Common uses
Stitching and finishing seams on knit fabrics for T-shirts, leggings, swimsuits and lingerie

Presser foot
Overcast, as the pin in it folds the narrow fabric edge flat to prevent the edge from rolling or bunching during stitching

Fabric type
Stretch knits

Thread type
Polyester

Needle type
Stretch or ballpoint

▶ SEE ALSO
Overcast foot, page 162

HOW TO SEW KNITS USING STRETCH OVEREDGE STITCH

1 Attach the overcast foot to your sewing machine and select the stretch overedge stitch. Insert a stretch or ballpoint needle.

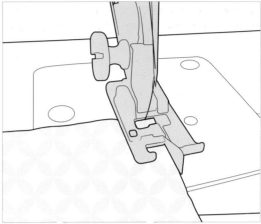

2 Position the fabric under the presser foot so that the right edge of the fabric is butting up against the guide on the foot. Lower the presser foot.

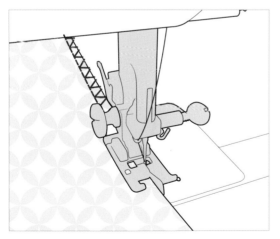

3 Using the guide on the foot as your seam guide, stitch the seam, making sure you backstitch at the beginning and end.

4 The stitches should go just off the edge of the fabric, on the right side.

 EXPERT TIP Be careful not to stretch the fabric as you are sewing, as this will cause it to distort and ripple.

Double Overedge Stitch

The double overedge stitch has two sets of overlapping zigzag stitches on the right and a straight stitch on the left. Sometimes the zigzag stitches are different sizes. This stitch is designed for overcasting the raw edges of fabrics that are prone to fraying. It is perfect for linen, shantung, gabardine and denim. It can be used to stitch and finish a seam in one operation. If using it to seam, make sure you trim your seam allowances to 6mm (¼in) before stitching. The double overedge stitch is available on many mechanical machines and most computerised sewing machines.

ESSENTIAL FACTS

Also known as
Serger stitch and overcast stitch

Key feature
Combination of a straight stitch and overlapping zigzags

Substitute stitch
Zigzag stitch, overcast stitch or slant pin stitch

Common uses
To finish raw edges to prevent fraying

Presser foot
Overcast

Fabric type
Woven fabrics that fray easily

Thread type
All-purpose polyester or cotton

Needle type
Universal, size appropriate for fabric

▶ SEE ALSO
Overcast foot, page 162

HOW TO FINISH A SEAM USING THE DOUBLE OVEREDGE STITCH

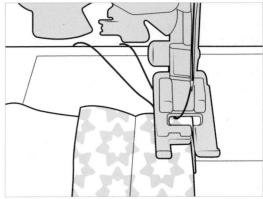

1 Sew the seam as usual and press the seam allowances open. Attach the overcast foot to the sewing machine and select the double overedge stitch.

2 Fold back the fabric so that you have one seam allowance and position the fabric under the presser foot so that the right fabric edge of the seam allowance is butting up against the guide on the foot. Lower the presser foot.

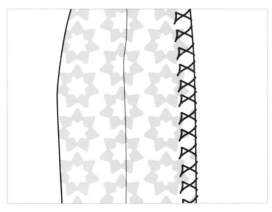

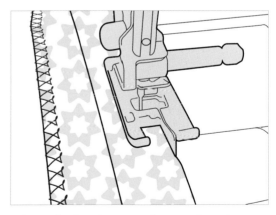

3 Overcast the seam, making sure you backstitch at the beginning and end. Use the guide on the foot as your seam guide. The stitches should go just off the edge on the right side.

4 Repeat for the other seam allowance. Press the seams open.

 EXPERT TIP It is also possible to overcast the seam allowances together. If you do this, press the seam allowances to one side instead of pressing them open.

Closed Overlock Stitch

The closed overlock stitch is another type of stitch that mimics a serger stitch and can be used for seaming and overcasting knit fabrics in one step. It can also be used to hem knits and give them a sporty look. It is ideal for stitching elastics directly on to fabric on waistbands as opposed to having elastic threaded through a casing. It has a stretch straight stitch on both the left and right sides, with zigzag stiches in between. Be sure to trim seam allowances to 6mm (1/4in) prior to sewing. The closed overlock stitch is commonly available on both mechanical and computerised sewing machines.

ESSENTIAL FACTS

Also known as
Overlock stitch, serger stitch and flatlock stitch

Key feature
Parallel straight stitches with zigzag in between

Substitute stitch
Stretch overedge stitch, slant pin stitch
or three-step zigzag stitch

Common uses
Seaming and hemming knits and applying elastic

Presser foot
Overcast for seam finishes; all-purpose for
applying elastic; walking for hemming knits

Fabric type
Stretch knits

Thread type
All-purpose polyester

Needle type
Stretch needle or ballpoint needle

▶ SEE ALSO
Stretch overedge stitch, page 48

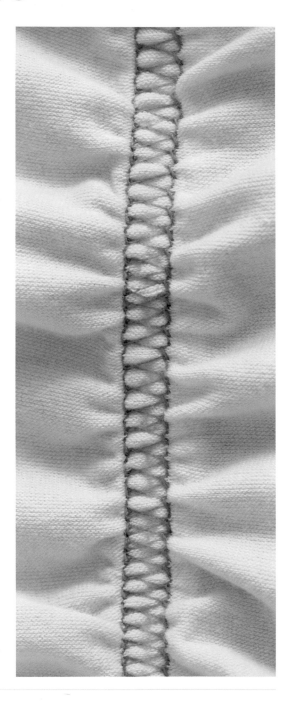

HOW TO APPLY ELASTIC USING THE CLOSED OVERLOCK STITCH

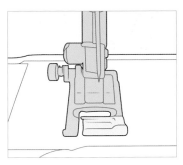

1 Attach the all-purpose foot to the sewing machine, select a zigzag stitch with a length of 2.5mm and a width of 2mm and insert a stretch/ballpoint needle.

2 Cut the elastic to the correct length, overlap the ends of the elastic by 13mm (1/2in) and stitch to form a circle.

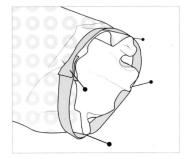

3 Quarter mark the elastic and quarter mark the garment at the centre front, centre back and side seams. Pin the elastic to the right side of the fabric, aligning along the right edge, matching each of the quarter-mark points, and pin at the points.

4 Position the elastic so it is centred under the presser foot. Select the closed overlock stitch.

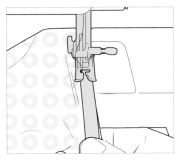

5 Backstitch and then stitch across the elastic, stretching flat from pin to pin. Backstitch at the end.

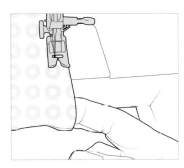

6 Turn elastic to the wrong side and again match and pin the quarter points. Position the fabric under the presser foot with the right side face up and the fabric fold against the right edge of the presser foot. Stitch across, stretching flat from pin to pin, making sure you backstitch at the beginning and end.

 EXPERT TIP 'Quarter mark' means to divide into four equal sections and mark with a pin.

Slant Pin Stitch

The slant pin stitch is an overcasting stitch for knit fabrics and is used to stitch seams and finish them in one step. It uses both forward and reverse stitches to allow maximum elasticity on highly stretchy fabrics. It has a stretch straight stitch on the left side and angled stiches on the right. Some slant pin stitches angle forward while on other machines they angle back. Like other overcast stitches, this stitch is only ¼in (6 mm) wide so be sure you trim the seam allowances prior to stitching. The slant pin stitch is available on most mechanical and all computerised sewing machines.

ESSENTIAL FACTS

Also known as
Knit overcast stitch and slant overedge stitch

Key feature
Combination of a straight stitch and overcast stitch

Substitute stitch
Stretch overedge stitch or closed overlock stitch

Common uses
Stitching and finishing seams on knit fabrics

Presser foot
Overcast

Fabric type
Stretch knits

Thread type
All-purpose polyester

Needle type
Stretch or ballpoint

▶ SEE ALSO
Overcast foot, page 162

HOW TO SEW KNITS USING THE SLANT PIN STITCH

1 Attach the overcast foot to the sewing machine and select the slant pin stitch. Insert a stretch/ballpoint needle in the machine.

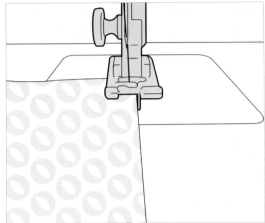

2 Position the fabric under the presser foot so that the right fabric edge is butting up against the guide on the foot. Lower the presser foot.

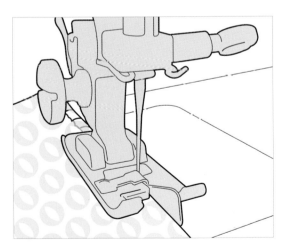

3 Stitch the seam, making sure you backstitch at the beginning and end. Use the guide on the foot as your seam guide.

4 The stitches should go just off the edge on the right side.

 EXPERT TIP You can also use the slant pin stitch to hem knits.

Reverse Overcast Stitch

The reverse overcast stitch has a stretch straight stitch on the right and zigzags on the left. Use it to apply overcast raw edges on knit fabrics, to apply lace trims and elastics to lingerie and as a decorative hem stitch on knits. Use with a stretch needle and polyester thread for knit fabrics and a universal or Microtex needle for delicate wovens. Be careful when using an overcasting foot, as on some machines the stitch pattern can make the needle hit the centre pin and break. You can also use an all-purpose or walking foot.

ESSENTIAL FACTS

Also known as
Reverse overedge stitch

Key feature
Reverse combination of a straight stitch and overcast stitch

Substitute stitch
Zigzag stitch

Common uses
Overcast knit fabrics, applying lace and elastic trim

Presser foot
Overcast, all-purpose or walking

Fabric type
Stretch knits, lace and elastics

Thread type
All-purpose polyester

Needle type
Stretch for knits; universal or Microtex for wovens

▶ SEE ALSO
All-purpose foot, page 158;
Walking foot, page 159

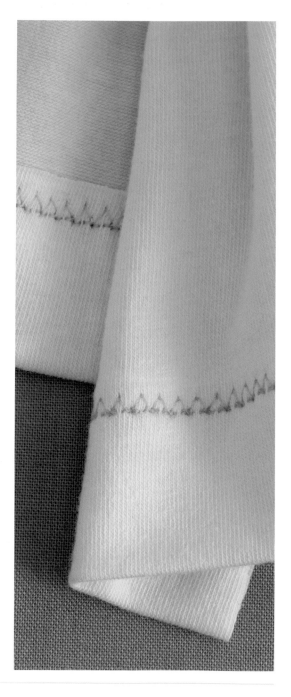

HOW TO HEM KNITS USING THE REVERSE OVERCAST STITCH

  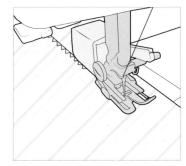

1 Press the full amount of the hem allowance to the wrong side; use an adjustable seam guide or tape measure for accuracy. Pin.

2 Attach the walking foot to the machine and select the reverse overcast stitch. Insert a stretch/ballpoint needle in the machine.

3 Position the fabric under the presser foot and align the fold on a seam guide that is the same measurement as the hem allowance. Lower the presser foot and stitch the hem, making sure you backstitch at the beginning and end.

HOW TO APPLY LACE TRIM USING THE REVERSE OVERCAST STITCH

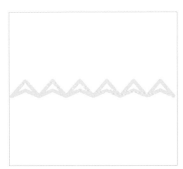 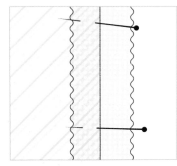 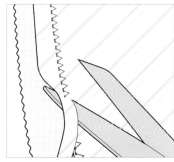

1 Attach the all-purpose foot to the sewing machine and select the reverse overcast stitch.

2 Pin the lace trim to the fabric's right side, overlapping the fabric raw edge by about 13mm (1/2in). Position the fabric under the presser foot so the lace edge is centred under the foot. Lower the presser foot.

3 Stitch along the lace edge, making sure you backstitch at the beginning and end. Trim away the excess fabric under the lace near the stitch line.

 EXPERT TIP You can also use the reverse overcast stitch to appliqué.

Shell Stitch

The shell stitch is used to create delicate shell tucks along folds. It has several straight stitches on the left and a straight stitch off to the right that pulls in the fold to form a slight tuck. The tension will need to be tightened for this stitch to create prominent tucks. Shell stitch is often used to hem lingerie and delicate knitwear and is beautiful along necklines. It is best used with lightweight fabrics that have some stretch or are on the bias. The shell stitch is available on some computerised sewing machines but is frequently substituted with overcast stitch.

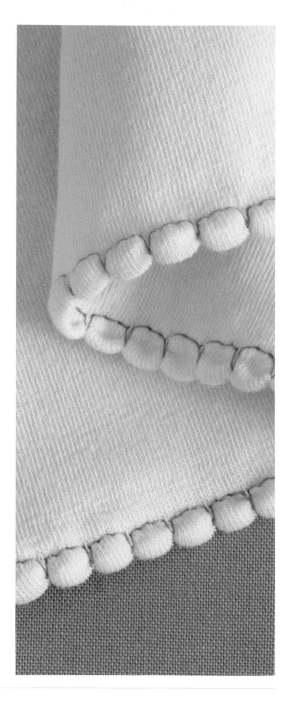

ESSENTIAL FACTS

Also known as
Picot edge stitch

Key feature
Several straight stitches on the left and one straight stitch off to the right

Substitute stitch
Overcast stitch

Common uses
Hems on knitwear and lingerie

Presser foot
Satin stitch

Fabric type
Knits and lightweight wovens

Thread type
Polyester for knits, cotton or polyester for wovens

Needle type
Universal for wovens; stretch for knits

▶ SEE ALSO
Satin stitch foot, page 158

HOW TO HEM KNITS USING SHELL STITCH

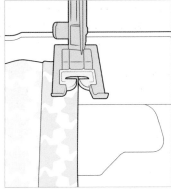

1 Press the hem 13mm (¹/₂in) to the wrong side. Use an adjustable seam guide or tape measure for accuracy. Pin.

2 Attach the satin stitch foot to the sewing machine and select the overcast stitch. Insert a stretch/ballpoint needle in the machine.

3 Position the fabric under the presser foot so that the fold is aligned with the centre guide of the presser foot.

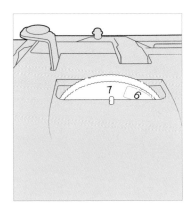

4 Tighten the tension to 7.

5 Lower the presser foot and stitch the edge. The zigzag should drop off the fabric edge and pull it in to the left to form the shell tuck. Be sure you backstitch at the beginning and end.

 EXPERT TIP If you want to create a more pronounced tuck, increase the tension.

The shell stitch can also be used to make a scalloped piping. You can use prepackaged bias tape or you can make your own. The benefit of making your own bias trim is that you can use any fabric, colour or pattern you desire.

HOW TO MAKE SCALLOPED PIPING USING SHELL STITCH

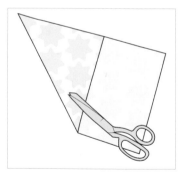

1 Fold the selvedge over to form a triangle, creating a 45-degree fold along the bias. Cut along that fold.

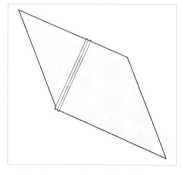

2 Pin the triangle to the other selvedge with right sides facing and stitch with a 6mm (¹/₄in) seam allowance. Press the seam allowances open and you will have a parallelogram.

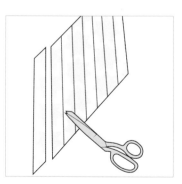

3 Using a ruler and a fabric marker, mark parallel lines to the bias edge that are 5cm (2in) apart. Cut on the lines using scissors or a rotary cutter, acrylic ruler and mat.

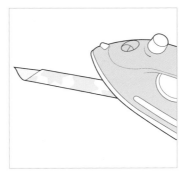

4 Place two strips of fabric right sides together at 90 degrees. Offset the tip of each strip by 6mm (1/4in). Pin. Select a straight stitch, length 2.5mm. Stitch with a 6mm seam allowance. Repeat until you have one long piece. Press the seam allowances open.

5 Fold the strip in half with the wrong sides facing and the long edges aligned. Press.

6 Attach the satin stitch foot to the sewing machine and select the overcast stitch. Tighten the tension to 7.

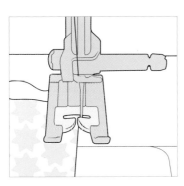

7 Position the fabric under the presser foot so that the fold is aligned with the centre guide of the presser foot.

8 Lower the presser foot and stitch along the folded edge. The zigzag should drop off the fabric edge and pull it in to the left to form the shell tuck. Always backstitch at the beginning and end.

9 Place the scalloped trim right side facing the right side of the hem of the garment. Pin. Stitch with a straight stitch and a 13mm (1/2in) seam allowance. Finish the raw edge with an overcast stitch and turn right side out.

 EXPERT TIP Shell stitch can be used on a skirt or dress hem or try it on a neckline. Use it as a trim on a pillow.

Crescent Stitch

The crescent stitch uses zigzag stitches to create delicate scalloped edges on blouse, dress and skirt hems, collar edges and necklines. It can be used as a decorative topstitch. The crescent stitch is seen on most mechanical and computerised machines. On mechanical machines, adjust the stitch length to 0.5mm and the width to the widest setting; computerised machines will adjust the settings automatically. Use crescent stitch with the satin stitch foot; the deep groove allows the dense stitches to pass under it easily. Use matching all-purpose thread or decorative rayon and metallic threads.

ESSENTIAL FACTS

Also known as
Scallop stitch

Key feature
Satin stitches in a scallop pattern

Substitute stitch
Satin stitch or bead stitch

Common uses
Decorative edges

Presser foot
Satin stitch

Fabric type
Lightweight wovens

Thread type
All-purpose polyester or decorative

Needle type
Universal, Microtex, embroidery, or metallic

▶ SEE ALSO
Satin stitch foot, page 158

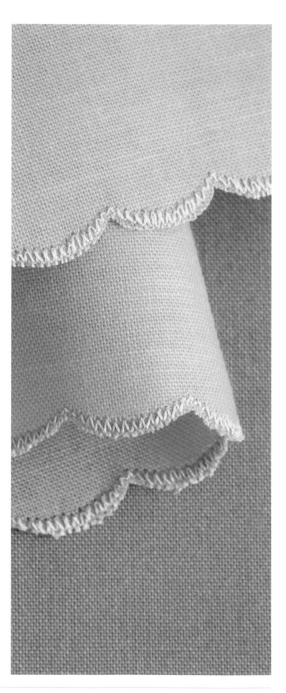

HOW TO STITCH A SCALLOPED EDGE USING CRESCENT STITCH

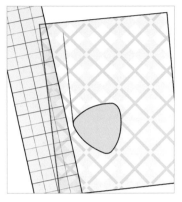

1 Spray starch and iron dry the fabric to stabilise it and prevent it from distorting during sewing. A tear-away stabiliser can also be used.

2 Draw a stitch guide on the right side of the fabric at the desired hem length using a ruler and tailor's chalk.

3 Install the satin stitch foot and select the crescent stitch. Adjust the stitch length and width if you need to.

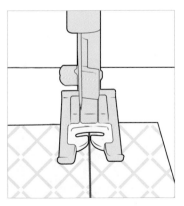

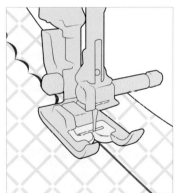

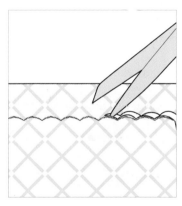

4 Position the fabric so the presser foot is centred on the chalk line and lower the presser foot.

5 Stitch the scalloped edge, making sure you secure the stitches at the beginning and end.

6 Cut away the excess fabric to the right of the stitches. Trim very close to the stitches without cutting through them.

 EXPERT TIP You can also use a twin needle to stitch a double crescent stitch. Using two different colours of thread adds an exciting decorative element to your project.

Serpentine Stitch

The serpentine stitch is a variation on the three-step zigzag stitch but it moves in a curved wave. It serves a similar purpose and is often used for mending tears and elastic application. This stitch is available on some mechanical machines and many computerised sewing machines. Use the all-purpose foot and polyester thread for applying elastic; polyester or cotton thread for mending or quilting; and a walking foot and cotton or decorative thread for quilting.

HOW TO APPLY ELASTIC USING THE SERPENTINE STITCH

1 Stretch the elastic the length of the seam and pin in place every 4 or 5cm, ensuring the elastic is evenly stretched.

2 Insert a stretch/ballpoint needle and select the serpentine stitch with a length of 2.5mm and width the same as the elastic. Position the elastic so it is centred under the presser foot.

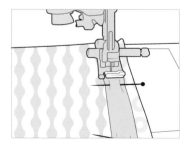

3 Backstitch and then stitch across the elastic, stretching flat from pin to pin. Backstitch at the end.

ESSENTIAL FACTS

Also known as
S stitch

Key feature
Wavy multi-stitch zigzag

Substitute stitch
Three-step zigzag stitch

Common uses
Attaching elastic, mending and topstitching on quilts

Presser foot
All-purpose or walking

Fabric type
All

Thread type
Polyester, cotton or decorative

Needle type
Universal for wovens; quilting for quilts; stretch for elastic

▶ SEE ALSO
Hand tacking, page 114

HOW TO QUILT USING SERPENTINE STITCH

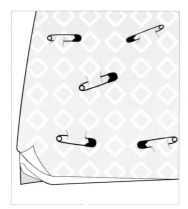

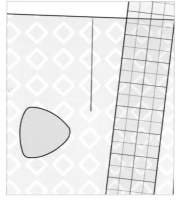

1 Assemble the quilt top. Layer the quilt back, wadding and quilt top Fix together by spray or hand tacking, or pin with safety pins.

2 Mark stitch lines on the quilt top using a fabric marker or tailor's chalk and ruler.

3 Install the walking foot on the machine. Insert a quilting needle and select the serpentine stitch.

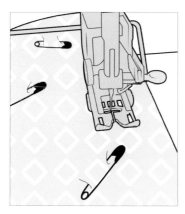

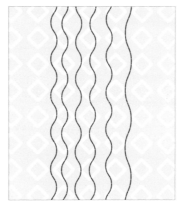

4 Place the fabric so that the first marked row is under the centre of the presser foot. Lower the presser foot and stitch the row.

5 Continue stitching each row in the same manner.

 EXPERT TIP Try adjusting the stitch length and width for different looks.

Fix Stitch

The fix stitch is a securing stitch to keep seams from unravelling. Rather than backstitching at the beginning and end of a seam, the sewing machine automatically takes several stitches in the same spot. Fix stitch is used where visible backstitching would be unattractive and is ideal for topstitching and appliqué. Most computerised sewing machines have this stitch.

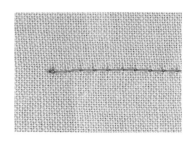

HOW TO TOPSTITCH USING FIX STITCH

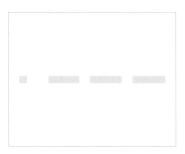

1 Sew the seam and press to one side. Select the fix stitch.

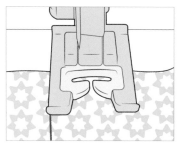

2 Position the fabric face up under the presser foot so that the seam is against the edge of the presser foot and the seam allowances are under the foot. Start stitching. The machine will stitch in the same place several times and then start stitching forward.

3 At the end, press the reverse button to lock the stitches.

 EXPERT TIP If your machine does not have a fix stitch, set it to a stitch length of 0mm and stitch the lock stitches. Then reset stitch length back to a standard stitch length of 2.5mm and stitch as usual.

ESSENTIAL FACTS

Also known as
Auto reinforcement

Key feature
Three to four securing stitches in the same spot

Substitute stitch
Backstitching

Common uses
Reinforces seams where visible backstitching is unwanted

Presser foot
All

Fabric type
All

Thread type
All

Needle type
All

▶ SEE ALSO
Straight stitch, page 10

Auto Backtack Stitch

The auto backtack stitch is a securing stitch to keep seams from unravelling and is available on computerised sewing machines. The machine automatically does several reverse stitches at the beginning and end of the seam.

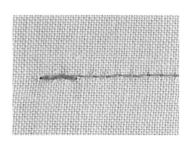

HOW TO SEW A SEAM USING AUTO BACKTACK STITCH

1 Lay the fabrics with the two right sides facing and pin. Select the auto backtack stitch and adjust stitch length to 2.5mm.

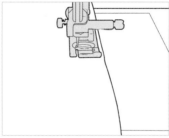

2 Line up the fabric on the appropriate seam guide and 6mm (1/4in) down from the top edge. Lower the presser foot. Press the reverse button and the machine will automatically stitch in reverse for several stitches and then stop.

3 Press the foot pedal and stitch forwards. At the end of the seam, press the reverse button, stitch several reverse stitches and stop.

EXPERT TIP In some cases computerised sewing machines can be programmed to do an auto reverse or fix stitch for any stitch.

ESSENTIAL FACTS

Also known as
Automatic backstitch

Key feature
Three to four reverse stitches at the beginning and the end of a seam

Substitute stitch
Backstitching

Common uses
Reinforces seams automatically

Presser foot
All

Fabric type
All

Thread type
All

Needle type
All

▶ SEE ALSO
Straight stitch, page 10

Bartack Stitch

The bartack stitch is a series of dense zigzag stitches that repeat back and forth several times. It is about 3mm (¹/₈in) wide and 13mm (¹/₂in) long but can be adjusted up to 28mm (1¹/₈in). It can be used as a reinforcement stitch in pocket openings, belt loops, fly zippers or purse straps, often in a contrasting colour to create a design element. A preprogrammed bartack stitch is often available on many computerised machines and is used with the automatic buttonhole foot to size the bartack. If you have a mechanical machine without a bartack stitch, use a basic zigzag with a stitch length of 0.5mm.

ESSENTIAL FACTS

Also known as
Reinforcement stitch

Key feature
Very dense zigzag stitches in one confined area

Substitute stitch
Zigzag

Common uses
Reinforce stress points to prevent rips

Presser foot
Automatic buttonhole

Fabric type
Wovens

Thread type
All-purpose polyester or topstitch

Needle type
Universal, topstitch or denim

▶ SEE ALSO
Hand bartack, page 132;
Automatic buttonhole foot, page 161

HOW TO STITCH A BARTACK

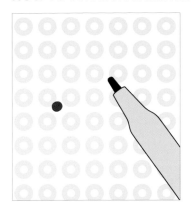

1 Mark the starting point for the bartack on the fabric with chalk or a fabric marker.

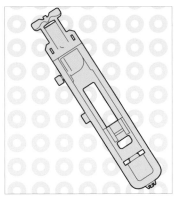

2 Then adjust the window on the automatic buttonhole foot to the length of the bartack and install the foot on the machine.

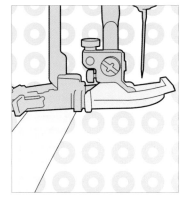

3 Lower the buttonhole lever so that it is between the two tabs on the left side of the foot.

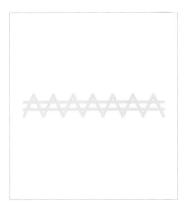

4 Select the bartack stitch.

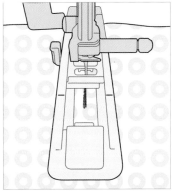

5 Position the foot so that you are starting at the bottom of the bartack. Lower the presser foot and start stitching. The machine will then stitch several straight stitches the length of the bartack.

6 Then it will stitch the zigzag stitches. At the end, the machine will do a couple of lock stitches to secure.

 EXPERT TIP The top and bottom of a machine-stitched buttonhole are also called bartacks.

Darning Stitch

Darning is the process of sewing rows of straight stitches close together to resemble woven fabric and is usually used to repair fabric tears or holes. Although traditionally done by hand, it is much faster to do by machine. Use thread in the closest possible colour match so that the repair is inconspicuous. Large tears should be backed with either a matching fabric or a lightweight fusible interfacing for stability. Backing is optional on small holes. The darning stitch is found on many computerised sewing machines and is used with the automatic buttonhole foot.

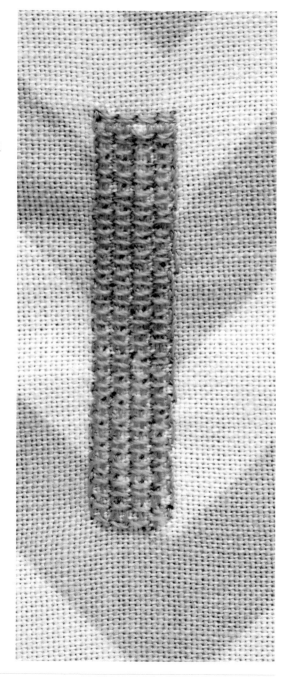

ESSENTIAL FACTS

Also known as
Mending stitch

Key feature
Tightly packed straight stitches

Substitute stitch
Three-step zigzag stitch or straight stitch

Common uses
Mending

Presser foot
Automatic buttonhole

Fabric type
Wovens

Thread type
Polyester or cotton in matching colour

Needle type
Universal

▶ SEE ALSO
Hand darning, page 128;
Buttonhole foot, page 161

HOW TO MEND A HOLE USING DARNING STITCH

1 Trim any frayed edges and back the hole with a piece of fusible interfacing that is 13mm (½in) bigger all the way around.

2 Using the automatic buttonhole foot, adjust the window to 6mm (¼in) longer than the length of the hole and install the foot on the machine.

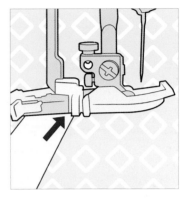

3 Lower the buttonhole lever so that it is between the two tabs on the left side of the foot.

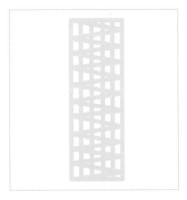

4 Select the darning stitch.

5 Position the foot so that you are starting at the bottom of the hole. Lower the presser foot and start stitching. The machine will stitch several columns of straight stitches up and down the length of the hole ending at the top.

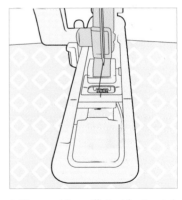

6 The machine will start horizontal rows of straight stitches and finish with a lockstitch.

 EXPERT TIP If the hole is wider than the darning stitch is programmed for, simply repeat the process for the unstitched portion.

Honeycomb Stitch

The honeycomb stitch consists of crisscrossing diagonal stitches. A hand-embroidery technique before the invention of elastic, smocking was often used to gather fabric around cuffs, bodices and necklines so that it could stretch. These days, it is generally done by machine. Used in children's clothing and lingerie, it is an heirloom sewing technique. The honeycomb stitch is also used for decorative topstitch, hemming, patchwork or appliqué and looks beautiful in a contrasting thread colour or in decorative embroidery threads. This common stitch is generally available on most mechanical and computerised machines.

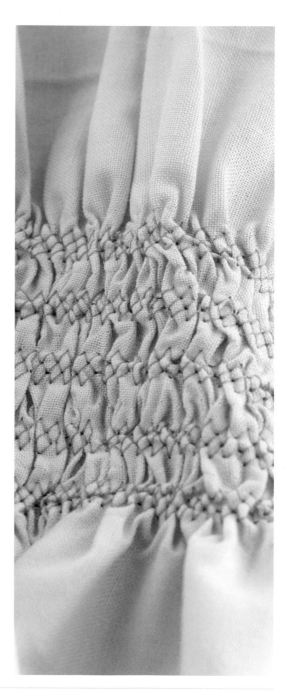

ESSENTIAL FACTS

Also known as
Smocking stitch

Key feature
Crisscrossing diagonal stitches

Substitute stitch
Feather stitch, faggoting stitch, Walls of Troy stitch or cross-stitch

Common uses
Gathered smocking, decorative stitches and appliqué

Presser foot
Satin stitch

Fabric type
Lightweight wovens

Thread type
Cotton, polyester or decorative

Needle type
Universal or embroidery

▶ SEE ALSO
Tacking stitch, page 16

HOW TO DO SMOCKING USING HONEYCOMB STITCH

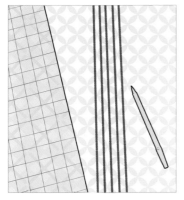

1 Cut the fabric three times wider than the desired finished width. Mark stitching lines across the width with a fabric marker or chalk every 13mm (1/2in).

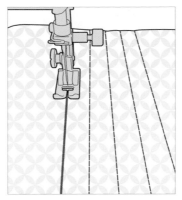

2 Set the machine to a tacking stitch or a straight stitch with a stitch length of at least 4mm. Loosen the tension to 1 or 2. Tack across the marked lines.

3 Pull on the bobbin thread to gather up the fabric. Tie the threads at either side of the fabric to secure.

4 Select the honeycomb stitch and reset the tension to 4. Thread the machine with decorative thread.

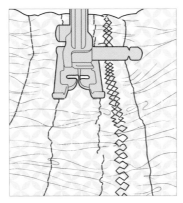

5 Stitch evenly spaced rows of the honeycomb stitch across the gathers between the rows of tacking stitches.

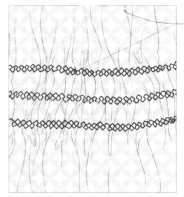

6 Remove the tacking stitches.

 EXPERT TIP Elastic shirring is often erroneously referred to as smocking. Elastic shirring makes similar-looking gathers using elastic thread and a straight stitch – see page 155.

Cross-stitch

The cross-stitch is designed to look like counted cross-stitch hand embroidery with X-shaped stitches in various repeating patterns. Often considered merely a decorative stitch, it is perfect for machine smocking. The X-shaped stitches have all the stretch and give of zigzag stitch and add a hand-worked look. Cross-stitch can also be used for topstitching, hemming, patchwork and appliqué. The cross-stitch is available on many computerised and some mechanical machines. All-purpose polyester or cotton threads are a good choice but decorative rayon or variegated threads make this stitch look more hand-stitched.

ESSENTIAL FACTS

Also known as
Sampler stitch

Key feature
Overlapping cross-stitches

Substitute stitch
Honeycomb, feather, faggoting and Walls of Troy

Common uses
Smocking, topstitching, hemming and decoration

Presser foot
Satin stitch

Fabric type
Wovens or knits

Thread type
Polyester, cotton or decorative

Needle type
Universal or embroidery

▶ SEE ALSO
Decorative threads, page 157

HOW TO DO SMOCKING USING CROSS-STITCH

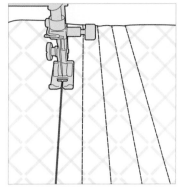

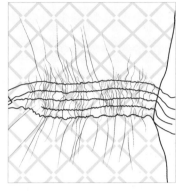

1 Cut the fabric three times wider than the desired finished width. Mark stitching lines across the width with a fabric marker or chalk every 13mm (1/2in).

2 Set the machine to a tacking stitch or a straight stitch with a stitch length of at least 4mm. Loosen the tension to 1 or 2. Tack across the marked lines.

3 Pull on the bobbin thread to gather up the fabric. Tie the threads at either side of the fabric to secure.

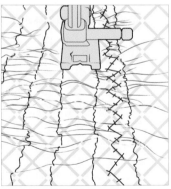

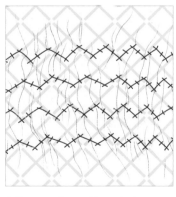

4 Select the cross-stitch and then reset the tension to 4. Thread the machine with the desired decorative thread.

5 Stitch rows of the cross-stitch across the gathers between the rows of tacking stitches.

6 Remove the tacking stitches.

 EXPERT TIP Some machines might even have a variety of cross-stitch patterns to choose from. Try using a different type of cross-stitch pattern on each row of smocking.

Walls of Troy Stitch

A variation of a zigzag pattern, Walls of Troy stitch is considered a decorative satin stitch; the stitches form an up-and-down step pattern. The shape is based on the silhouette of the walls of the ancient city of Troy. The Walls of Troy stitch is often used for smocking, topstitching, patchwork and appliqué. Traditionally, it has three steps but variations have four and five steps. It is available on many computerised sewing machines and on some mechanical machines. Use with all-purpose polyester or cotton threads, or choose decorative rayon or variegated threads.

ESSENTIAL FACTS

Also known as
Top hat stitch

Key feature
Zigzag stitches that form steps

Substitute stitch
Honeycomb, feather, cross-stitch or faggoting

Common uses
Topstitching, smocking, hemming and decoration

Presser foot
Satin stitch

Fabric type
Wovens or knits

Thread type
Polyester, cotton or decorative

Needle type
Universal or embroidery

▶ SEE ALSO
Decorative threads, page 157

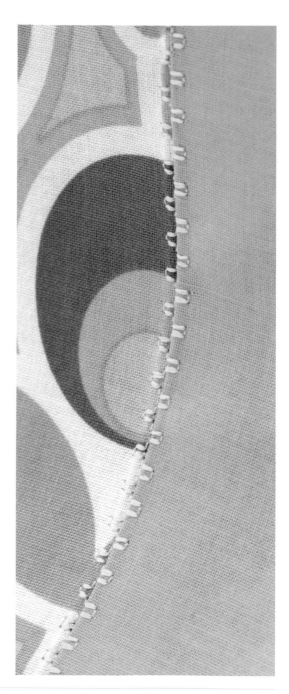

HOW TO TOPSTITCH USING WALLS OF TROY STITCH

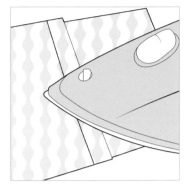

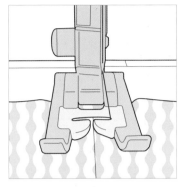

1 Using a basic straight stitch, sew seams in the usual manner and press them to one side.

2 Install the satin stitch foot, thread the machine with the desired thread and select the Walls of Troy stitch.

3 Position the fabric face up under the presser foot so that the seam edge is centred under the presser foot. Use the centre split as your seam guide. Make sure the seam allowances are under the foot so that you are stitching through all three layers. Lower the presser foot.

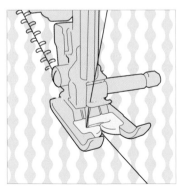

4 Stitch the seam, leaving long thread tails at the beginning and end instead of backstitching.

5 Using a hand needle, pull the top thread tails through to the wrong side of the fabric and hand tie off.

 EXPERT TIP Since the Walls of Troy stitch is a zigzag stitch, it can stretch, and therefore be used for hemming knits.

Feather Stitch

The feather stitch is intended to replicate hand embroidery and has diagonal stitches going left and right from the centre. It is very popular for crazy quilt patchwork. Feather stitch can be used as a decorative topstitch. Like many decorative stitches, it is a variation on a zigzag stitch and so can be used for stretch knits. It can also be used for faggoting, smocking and appliqué. The feather stitch is a very common stitch and is found on most sewing machines. Use with a contrasting thread colour for the best effect.

ESSENTIAL FACTS

Also known as
Briar stitch

Key feature
Diagonal stitches radiating from the centre

Substitute stitch
Honeycomb, cross-stitch or faggoting

Common uses
Patchwork, smocking, topstitching, hemming and faggoting

Presser foot
Satin stitch

Fabric type
Wovens

Thread type
Polyester, cotton or decorative

Needle type
Universal or embroidery

▶ SEE ALSO
Patchwork foot, page 163

HOW TO DO CRAZY QUILT PATCHWORK USING FEATHER STITCH

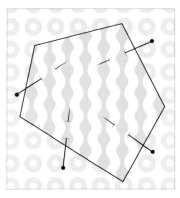

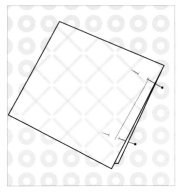

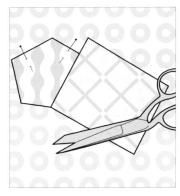

1 Cut a piece of muslin or flannel the size of the finished quilt block for the foundation. Cut an angled piece of fabric for the centre patch and pin onto the foundation block.

2 Install the patchwork foot. Take the next piece of fabric and lay it right sides facing with one side aligned with one side of the centre patch. Stitch edge with a straight stitch.

3 Flip the right side out and press. Trim excess fabric on either end.

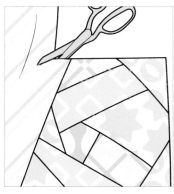

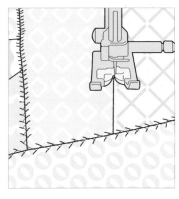

4 Stitch on next piece of fabric to that edge, flip and press. Repeat until block is complete. Trim any excess fabric that hangs beyond the foundation piece.

5 Select the feather stitch and install the satin stitch foot.

6 Work on the right side. Stitch on top of each seam, centring it under the presser foot. With a hand needle, pull top thread tails to the wrong side and hand tie off.

 EXPERT TIP You can make as many blocks as you like and then stitch them together and proceed as you would with any other quilt.

Faggoting Stitch

Faggoting is the technique of joining hemmed edges by crisscrossing thread over an open seam and creating a delicate lace effect. It is very popular in vintage clothing and adds a couture touch to any project. Try using it along a hem, across the top of a pocket or on linens. Most computerised machines have one or two stitches designed for this technique. The faggoting stitch itself is a novelty zigzag stitch with more flourish. It can also be used for decorative topstitch, hems, crazy-quilt patchwork, smocking and appliqué.

ESSENTIAL FACTS

Also known as
Bridging stitch

Key feature
Novelty zigzag stitch

Substitute stitch
Feather stitch

Common uses
Designed to stitch across open seams, decoration and appliqué

Presser foot
All-purpose

Fabric type
Wovens

Thread type
Topstitch

Needle type
Topstitch

▶ SEE ALSO
Topstitch needle, page 152;
Topstitch thread, page 156

HOW TO STITCH A FAGGOTED SEAM

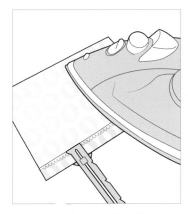

1 Overcast the raw edge of each seam and then fold under each edge 15mm (5/8in) and press.

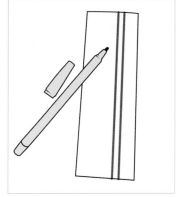

2 Take a piece of wash-away or tear-away stabiliser and draw two lines 3mm (1/8in) apart with a fabric marker or tailor's chalk.

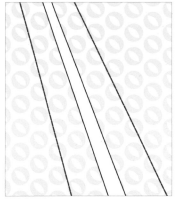

3 Tack the folded fabric edges to these lines, leaving a 3mm (1/8in) gap between the fabrics.

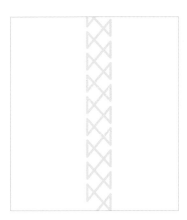

4 Select the faggoting stitch, install a topstitch needle, and thread the machine with topstitch thread.

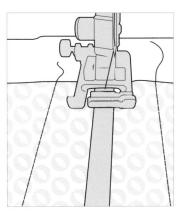

5 Position the fabric so the gap is centred under the presser foot.

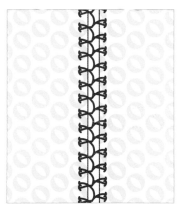

6 Stitch the open seam, making sure you catch each fold, and then remove the stabiliser according to the instructions.

 EXPERT TIP You can use lighter threads for a more delicate look. Try silk, rayon or cotton threads and use a Microtex needle or embroidery needle.

Rampart Stitch

The rampart stitch has several straight stitches, a zigzag to one side, then several more straight stitches on the other side. It is named after the defensive walls of old forts. It is a joining stitch designed to stitch over flat overlapped edges. Rampart stitch is frequently used to join pieces of sew-in interfacing since using a standard seam with seam allowances would create too much bulk. It can also be used for decorative topstitch, faggoting or crazy-quilt patchwork. The rampart stitch is found on most mechanical machines and most computerised sewing machines.

ESSENTIAL FACTS

Also known as
Box stitch

Key feature
Straight stitches combined with zigzag stitches

Substitute stitch
Three-step zigzag stitch, feather stitch
or faggoting stitch

Common uses
Stitching flat overlapped seams and
decorative stitching

Presser foot
All-purpose

Fabric type
Interfacing, wovens

Thread type
All-purpose polyester

Needle type
Universal

▶ SEE ALSO
All-purpose foot, page 158

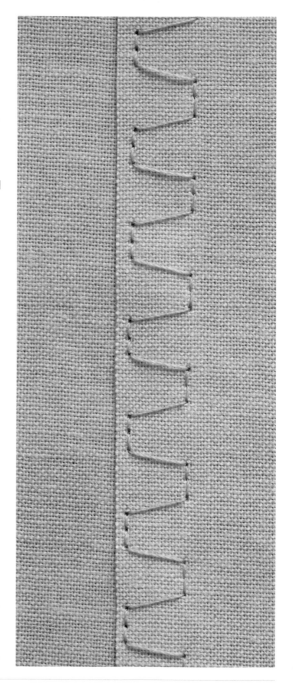

HOW TO JOIN EDGES USING RAMPART STITCH

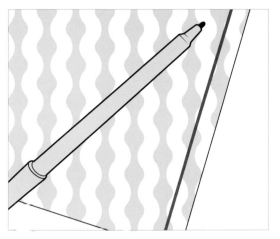

1 Use chalk or a fabric marker to mark a line 10mm (³/₈in) in from the edge on one piece of interfacing.

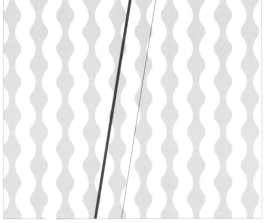

2 Align the edge of the other piece of interfacing onto this edge so they are overlapped by 10mm (³/₈in).

3 Select the rampart stitch and set the stitch length to 2.5mm.

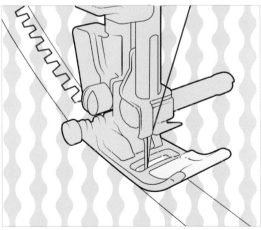

4 Align the fabric edge on the left edge of the presser foot, lower the presser foot, and stitch the seam. Be sure you backstitch at the beginning and end.

 EXPERT TIP Make sure you match the thread colour to the interfacing to ensure it doesn't show through the main fabric.

Appliqué Stitch

Appliqué stitch looks like a comb with straight stitches on the right and horizontal stitches to the left. Used to stitch appliqué patches onto a base fabric, the straight stitches are on the base and the horizontal stitches are on the appliqué. It can also be used as a decorative topstitch, to finish the edges of napkins and linens and also for patchwork. The appliqué stitch is available on most computerised sewing machines and usually has an auto backtack. Use it with the satin stitch foot or open toe foot. Match the thread colour to the appliqué or base fabric, or use a contrasting thread colour for impact.

ESSENTIAL FACTS

Also known as
Blanket stitch

Key feature
Straight stitch on the right and horizontal stitches on the left

Substitute stitch
Zigzag stitch or satin stitch

Common uses
Appliqué, topstitch, patchwork and decorative edging

Presser foot
Satin stitch

Fabric type
Wovens

Thread type
Polyester, cotton or embroidery

Needle type
Universal or embroidery

▶ SEE ALSO
Satin stitch foot, page 158;
Open toe foot, page 163

HOW TO APPLIQUÉ USING APPLIQUÉ STITCH

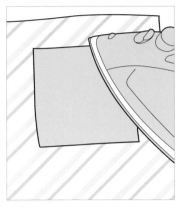

1 Following the manufacturer's instructions for iron temperature and time, apply fusible webbing to the wrong side of the fabric you are using to appliqué.

2 Using a fabric marker, draw the appliqué shape on the wrong side of the appliqué. Keep the shape simple. Cut out the appliqué on the line and peel off the paper.

3 Place the appliqué face up onto the fabric it will be stitched to and iron to hold in place.

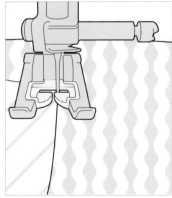

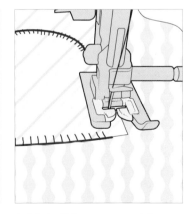

4 Install the satin stitch or open toe foot on the machine and select the appliqué stitch.

5 Position the fabric so that the needle comes down just outside the edge of the appliqué.

6 Stitch all the way around the appliqué, making sure you backtack at the beginning and end.

 EXPERT TIP When pivoting around outside angles (such as the bottom point of a heart), make sure the needle is down in the left-hand position. When stitching around an inside angle (such as between scallops) your needle should be down in the right-hand position.

Reverse Appliqué Stitch

Used where the top layer of fabric is cut away and the appliqué fabric is revealed below, reverse appliqué stitch looks like a comb with straight stitches on the left and horizontal stitches to the right. The straight stitches are on the appliqué and the horizontal stitches are on the main fabric. This stitch can be used as a decorative topstitch, for patchwork and also as a decorative edge. It is available on most computerised sewing machines. Use it with the satin stitch or the open toe foot. Match the thread colour to the appliqué or main fabric or use a contrasting colour for impact.

ESSENTIAL FACTS

Also known as
Reverse blanket stitch

Key feature
Straight stitch on the left and horizontal stitches on the right

Substitute stitch
Zigzag stitch or satin stitch

Common uses
Appliqué, topstitch, patchwork and decorative edging

Presser foot
Satin stitch

Fabric type
Wovens

Thread type
Polyester, cotton or embroidery

Needle type
Universal or embroidery

▶ SEE ALSO
Satin stitch foot, page 158; Open toe foot, page 163

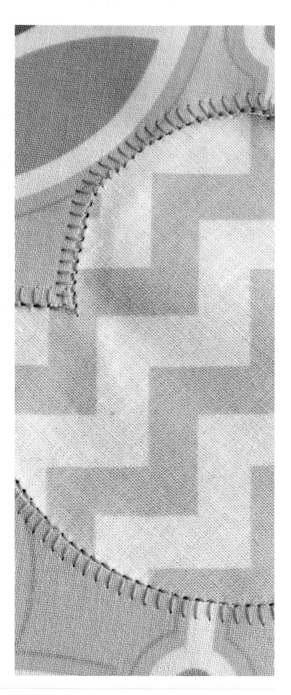

HOW TO REVERSE APPLIQUÉ USING REVERSE APPLIQUÉ STITCH

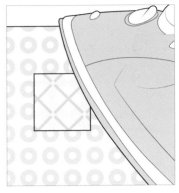

1 Apply fusible webbing to the wrong side of the main fabric, following the manufacturer's instructions for iron temperature and time. Make sure the webbing is at least 25mm (1in) bigger all the way around than the appliqué design.

2 Using a fabric marker, draw the appliqué shape on the wrong side of the main fabric. Cut out the appliqué on the line and peel off the paper.

3 Cut a patch of appliqué fabric that is at least 25mm (1in) bigger than the appliqué design. Place the main fabric face up onto the appliqué fabric and iron to hold in place.

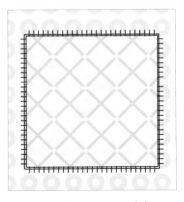

4 Install the satin stitch or open toe foot on the machine and select the reverse appliqué stitch.

5 Position the fabric so that the needle comes down just outside the edge of the main fabric.

6 Stitch all the way around the appliqué, taking care to backtack at the beginning and end.

 EXPERT TIP If your machine does not have a reverse appliqué stitch, use the mirror-image function to flip the appliqué stitch.

Asterisk Stitch

The asterisk stitch is a decorative pattern that mimics hand embroidery. As you sew, you make a continuous row of asterisks. Some computerised machines can be programmed to stitch a single asterisk. The stitch can often be used for appliqué or decorative topstitching. Try using it to stitch down a ribbon. It is popular as an heirloom stitch when paired with a wing needle. The asterisk stitch is usually available on most computerised machines and typically has an auto backtack. Use it with the satin stitch foot to allow for the heavy build-up of stitches. Match the thread or use a contrasting colour for impact.

ESSENTIAL FACTS

Also known as
Star stitch and daisy stitch

Key feature
Star-shaped stitches

Substitute stitch
Satin stitch, decorative motifs or zigzag

Common uses
Heirloom hemstitch, appliqué and decorative stitching

Presser foot
Satin stitch

Fabric type
Wovens

Thread type
Polyester, cotton or embroidery

Needle type
Universal, embroidery or wing

▶ SEE ALSO
Satin stitch foot, page 158

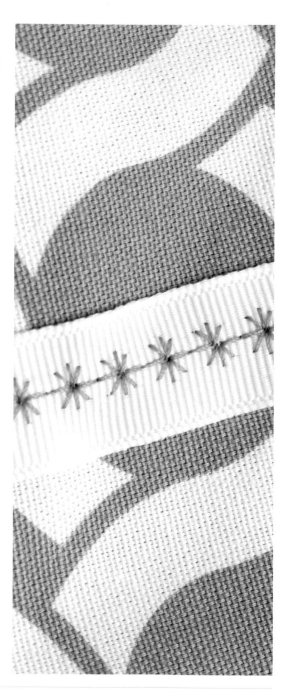

HOW TO TOPSTITCH A RIBBON USING ASTERISK STITCH

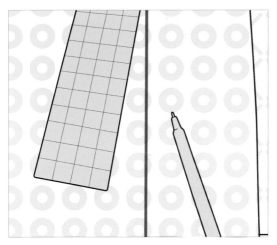

1 Using a fabric marker or tailor's chalk, draw a line on the fabric as a placement guide for the ribbon.

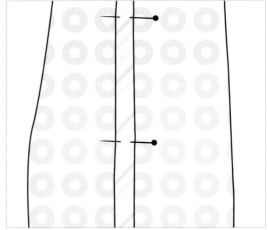

2 Pin the ribbon to the fabric, aligning on the marker line.

3 Select the asterisk stitch and install the satin stitch foot. Thread the machine with the desired thread.

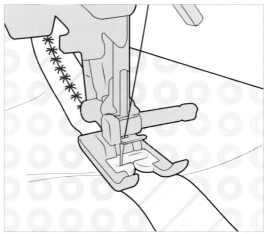

4 Stitch down the ribbon, making sure you backtack at the beginning and end.

 EXPERT TIP It is best to embellish fabric with ribbon before you construct the project. That way, the ribbon ends will be hidden in the seams.

Ladder Stitch

The ladder stitch has two parallel rows of straight stitches with stitches going straight across in between. It can be used for faggoting, decorative topstitching and patchwork. Ladder stitch also looks beautiful with a narrow ribbon threaded through it. It is available on most computerised machines and typically has an auto backtack. Use it with the satin stitch foot to allow for the heavy build-up of stitches. Match the thread colour or use a contrasting thread colour for an additional design element.

ESSENTIAL FACTS

Also known as
Bridging stitch

Key feature
Parallel straight stitches with horizontal stitch in between

Substitute stitch
Zigzag stitch or faggoting stitch

Common uses
Topstitch, patchwork, ribbon threading and faggoting

Presser foot
Satin stitch or open toe foot

Fabric type
Wovens

Thread type
Polyester, cotton, topstitch or embroidery

Needle type
Universal, topstitch or embroidery

▶ SEE ALSO
Satin stitch foot, page 158;
Open toe foot, page 163

HOW TO DO RIBBON THREADING USING LADDER STITCH

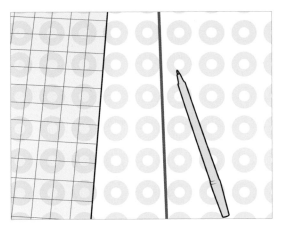

1 Using a fabric marker or tailor's chalk, draw a line on the fabric as a placement guide for the stitching.

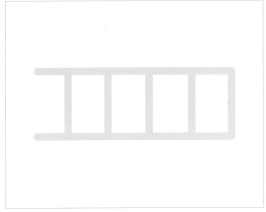

2 Select the ladder stitch and install the satin stitch foot. Thread the machine with the desired thread.

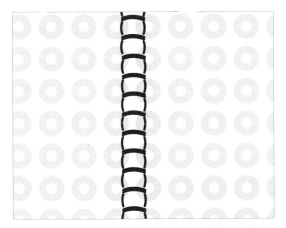

3 Centre the drawn line under the presser foot and stitch down the line making sure you backtack at the beginning and at the end. Repeat for additional rows if desired.

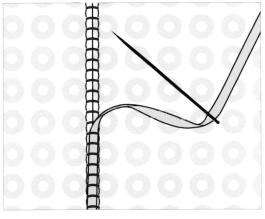

4 Thread the ribbon through a large needle such as a tapestry or sack needle. Use the needle to thread the ribbon under the horizontal stitches of the ladder stitch. Secure the ribbon ends with small hand stitches or fabric glue.

 EXPERT TIP Instead of threading under each stitch, try threading under every other stitch for a different look.

Lattice Stitch

The lattice stitch has two parallel rows of straight stitches with zigzag stitches going across in between. Used as an heirloom stitch on tightly woven fabrics such as linen, lawn and batiste, it is sewn with a wing needle. The flanges on the sides of the wing needle create a large hole with each stitch that is held open with the stitches. It adds a delicate vintage look to lingerie, blouses and dresses. The lattice stitch is available on most computerised machines and typically with an auto backtack. Use it with the satin stitch foot. Match the thread colour to the fabric or use a contrasting thread as a design feature.

ESSENTIAL FACTS

Also known as
Heirloom stitch

Key feature
Heavy parallel straight stitches with zigzag
in between

Substitute stitch
Double triangle stitch, pin stitch or asterisk stitch

Common uses
Heirloom stitch

Presser foot
Satin stitch or open toe

Fabric type
Tightly woven fabric such as linen, lawn and batiste

Thread type
Cotton or embroidery

Needle type
Wing

▶ SEE ALSO
Wing needle, page 152

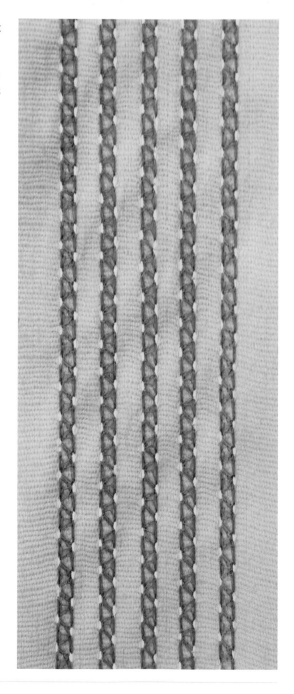

HOW TO SEW AN HEIRLOOM STITCH USING LATTICE STITCH

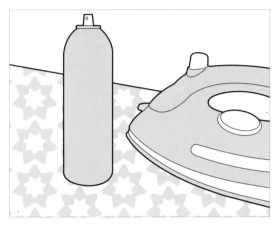

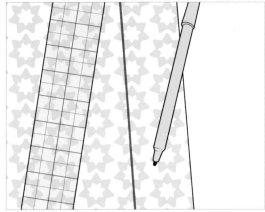

1 Mist the fabric with spray starch and iron dry. Repeat several times so that the fabric is very stiff.

2 Mark a stitching line on the fabric with a fabric marker or tailor's chalk.

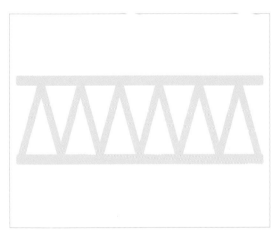

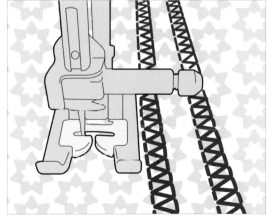

3 Install the satin stitch foot and a wing needle, thread the machine with the desired thread, and select the lattice stitch.

4 Centre the drawn line under the presser foot and stitch down the line making sure you backtack at the beginning and at the end. Repeat for additional rows if desired.

 EXPERT TIP Always do a test swatch to make sure the fabric marker or chalk will wash out.

Pin Stitch

The pin stitch looks like a reverse appliqué stitch with straight stitches on the left and horizontal stitches to the right. But it is heavier; the needle repeats each stitch several times. It is designed to be an heirloom hemstitch on natural-fibre woven fabric such as lawn, linen and batiste, and is sewn with a wing needle. Although traditionally sewn in white on white fabric, use any thread colour for a modern look. The pin stitch is available on most computerised sewing machines and normally has an auto backtack. Use it with the satin stitch foot to allow for the heavy build-up of stitches.

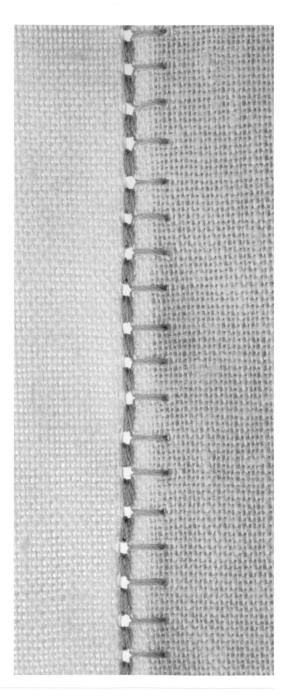

ESSENTIAL FACTS

Also known as
Picot stitch and Parisian hemstitch

Key feature
Heavy straight vertical stitches with horizontal stitches to the right

Substitute stitch
Double triangle stitch, ladder stitch or asterisk stitch

Common uses
Heirloom stitch

Presser foot
Satin stitch or open toe

Fabric type
Tightly woven fabric, such as linen, lawn and batiste

Thread type
Cotton or embroidery

Needle type
Wing

▶ SEE ALSO
Wing needle, page 152

HOW TO SEW AN HEIRLOOM HEMSTITCH USING PIN STITCH

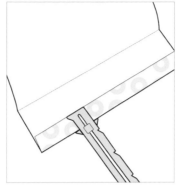

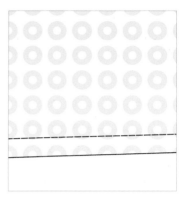

1 Mist the fabric with spray starch and iron dry. Repeat several times so that the fabric is very stiff.

2 Press the hem to the wrong side the full amount of your hem allowance. Use a seam gauge or tape measure to make sure it's accurate. Unfold and turn the raw edge under 6mm (¹/₄in) and press again. Refold and pin the hem for sewing.

3 Next, tack the hem in place 6mm (¹/₄in) away from the folded edge.

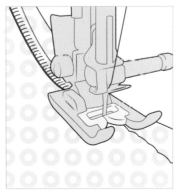

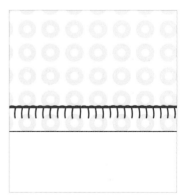

4 Install the satin stitch foot and a wing needle, thread the machine with the desired thread, and select the pin stitch.

5 Stitch down the fold, making sure you backtack at the beginning and end.

6 Remove the tacking stitch.

 EXPERT TIP You can add extra rows of pin stitches or lattice stitches for additional interest.

Double Triangle Stitch

The double triangle stitch has triangle stitches on both sides of a straight centre stitch. A heavy heirloom stitch, the needle repeats each stitch several times. It is used on tightly woven fabrics such as linen, lawn and batiste, and sewn with a wing needle. It is often used to make *entredeux*, a machine-embroidered trim with open holes sewn between rows of lace. It can be used either as an heirloom hem or a topstitch. Available on most computerised sewing machines, it typically has an auto backtack. Use it with the satin stitch or open toe foot. Match the thread to the fabric or use a contrasting colour.

ESSENTIAL FACTS

Also known as
Entredeux and Venetian hemstitch

Key feature
Heavy triangle stitches on both sides of a straight centre stitch

Substitute stitch
Ladder, pin stitch or asterisk stitch

Common uses
Heirloom stitch

Presser foot
Satin stitch or open toe

Fabric type
Tightly woven fabric, such as linen and batiste

Thread type
Cotton or embroidery

Needle type
Wing

▶ SEE ALSO
Wing needle, page 152

HOW TO SEW LACE USING DOUBLE TRIANGLE STITCH

1 Mist the fabric with spray starch and iron dry. Repeat several times so that the fabric is very stiff.

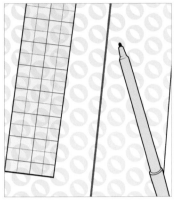

2 Mark a guide line for the lace on the fabric with a fabric marker or tailor's chalk.

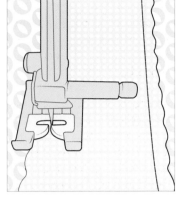

3 Tack the lace in place along both edges.

4 Install the satin stitch foot, thread the machine with the desired thread and select the double triangle stitch.

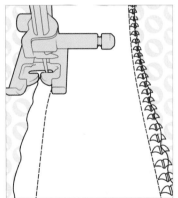

5 Centre the edge of the lace under the presser foot and stitch down the line, making sure you backtack at the beginning and end. Repeat for the other edge of the lace.

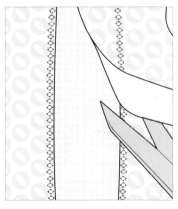

6 Cut away the excess fabric beneath the lace.

 EXPERT TIP Try using the double triangle stitch instead of topstitching around a collar, across the top of a pocket or along a shoulder seam.

Quilt Stitch

The quilt stitch resembles a handsewn running stitch. It alternates the triple straight stitch with the standard straight stitch and is most often used to topstitch both quilts and bindings. It can also be used to topstitch when you want to create a hand-stitched look. Use quilt stitch to topstitch a hem, collar or pocket, or to stitch on trims and ribbons. The quilt stitch is available on most computerised sewing machines and has an auto backtack. Use a walking foot and cotton or decorative thread for quilting. When topstitching, use polyester or topstitching thread.

ESSENTIAL FACTS

Also known as
Running stitch and hand-look stitch

Key feature
Heavy straight stitch that resembles a hand stitch

Substitute stitch
Straight stitch or stretch straight stitch

Common uses
Quilting and topstitching

Presser foot
All-purpose or walking

Fabric type
Wovens

Thread type
Polyester, cotton or decorative

Needle type
Quilting, universal or topstitch

▶ SEE ALSO
Running stitch, page 112

HOW TO QUILT USING QUILT STITCH

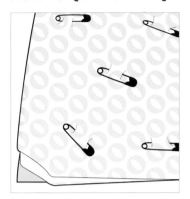

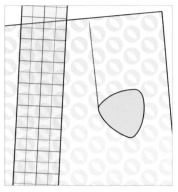

1 Assemble the quilt top and then put together the quilt sandwich by layering the quilt top, wadding and quilt back. Tack together by spray tacking or hand tacking, or use safety pins.

2 Mark stitch lines on the quilt top using a fabric marker or tailor's chalk and a ruler.

3 Install the walking foot on the machine and insert a quilting needle. Select the quilt stitch.

4 Position the fabric so that your first marked row is under the centre of the presser foot. Lower the presser foot and stitch the row, backtacking at the beginning and end.

5 Continue stitching each row in the same manner.

 EXPERT TIP The quilt stitch is also charming on appliqués. Fold the raw edges under 6mm (¹/₄in), press and stitch in place using the quilt stitch.

Arrowhead Stitch

The arrowhead stitch is a triangle-shaped satin stitch. Use it to stitch appliqués, topstitch or stitch on trims. It is found on many computerised and mechanical machines. On a mechanical machine, adjust the stitch length to 0.5mm, the width to 4mm, and secure the stitches at the beginning and end of each seam. Computerised machines make these adjustments automatically and have an auto backtack.

HOW TO APPLIQUÉ USING ARROWHEAD STITCH

1 Place the appliqué face up onto the fabric and pin in place.

2 Select the arrowhead stitch, install the satin stitch foot, and thread the machine with the desired thread.

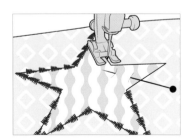

3 Line up the end of the appliqué with the centre of the presser foot and stitch around it.

EXPERT TIP In some cases computerised sewing machines allow you to mirror image the stitch so that the triangles point down instead of up.

ESSENTIAL FACTS

Also known as
Triangle stitch

Key feature
Triangle-shaped satin stitch

Substitute stitch
Zigzag

Common uses
Decorative topstitch
and appliqué

Presser foot
Satin stitch or open toe

Fabric type
All

Thread type
Polyester, cotton or embroidery

Needle type
Universal or embroidery

▶ SEE ALSO
Satin stitch foot, page 158

Banner Stitch

The banner stitch is a satin stitch made by zigzags to form flag shapes. Use it to stitch appliqués, topstitch or stitch on trims. The banner stitch is found on many computerised and mechanical machines. On a mechanical machine, adjust the stitch length to 0.5mm, the width to 4mm, and secure the stitches at the beginning and end of each seam. Computerised sewing machines make these adjustments automatically and have an auto backtack.

HOW TO HEM USING BANNER STITCH

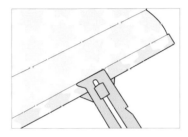

1 Using a seam gauge or tape measure to ensure accuracy, press the full amount of your hem allowance to the wrong side. Unfold and turn the raw edge under 6mm (¹/₄in) and press again. Refold and hand-tack hem for sewing.

2 Install the satin stitch foot, thread the machine with the desired thread and select the banner stitch.

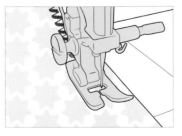

 EXPERT TIP You may need to stabilise the fabric when satin stitching – use spray starch or tear-away stabiliser.

3 Stitch down the fold making sure to backtack at the beginning and end. Remove the tacking stitches.

ESSENTIAL FACTS

Also known as
Flag stitch

Key feature
Flag-shaped satin stitch

Substitute stitch
Zigzag

Common uses
Decorative topstitch and appliqué

Presser foot
Satin stitch or open toe

Fabric type
All

Thread type
Polyester, cotton or embroidery

Needle type
Universal or embroidery

▶ SEE ALSO
Hand-tacking stitch, page 114

Bead Stitch

The bead stitch is an oval-shaped satin stitch. Use it to stitch appliqués, topstitch or trims. It is found on many computerised and mechanical machines. On a mechanical machine, adjust the stitch length to 0.5mm, the width to 4mm, and secure the stitches at the beginning and end of each seam. Computerised machines make these adjustments automatically and have an auto backtack.

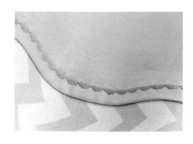

HOW TO TOPSTITCH USING BEAD STITCH

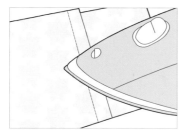

1 Using a basic straight stitch, sew seams and press to one side.

2 Install the satin stitch foot and thread machine with the desired thread. Select the bead stitch.

3 Position the fabric face up under the presser foot so that the seam edge is against the edge of the presser on the foot. Make sure the seam allowances are under the foot so that you are stitching through all three layers. Lower the presser foot and stitch.

EXPERT TIP In some cases computerised sewing machines will allow you to elongate the design without spreading out the stitches.

ESSENTIAL FACTS

Also known as
Rounded satin stitch

Key feature
Oval-shaped satin stitch

Substitute stitch
Zigzag

Common uses
Decorative topstitch and appliqué

Presser foot
Satin stitch or open toe

Fabric type
All

Thread type
Polyester, cotton or embroidery

Needle type
Universal or embroidery

▶ SEE ALSO
Satin stitch foot, page 158

Diamond Stitch

The diamond stitch is a kite-shaped satin stitch. The diamond stitch is found on many computerised and mechanical machines. On a mechanical machine, adjust the stitch length to 0.5mm, the width to 4mm, and secure the stitches at the beginning and end of each seam. Computerised machines make these adjustments automatically and have an auto backtack.

HOW TO STITCH A RIBBON USING DIAMOND STITCH

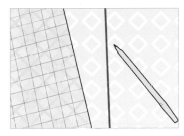

1 Using a fabric marker or tailor's chalk, draw a line on the fabric as a placement guide for the ribbon. Pin the ribbon to the fabric, aligning on the marker line.

2 Select the diamond stitch and install the satin stitch foot. Thread the machine with the desired thread.

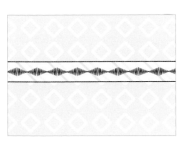

3 Stitch down the ribbon, making sure to backtack at the beginning and end.

ESSENTIAL FACTS

Also known as
Kite stitch

Key feature
Diamond-shaped satin stitch

Substitute stitch
Zigzag

Common uses
Decorative topstitch and appliqué

Presser foot
Satin stitch or open toe

Fabric type
All

Thread type
Polyester, cotton or embroidery

Needle type
Universal or embroidery

▶ SEE ALSO
Satin stitch foot, page 158

Domino Stitch

The domino stitch is a chequerboard satin stitch. Use it to stitch appliqués, topstitch hems or trims. The domino stitch is found on many computerised and mechanical machines. On a mechanical machine, adjust the stitch length to 0.5mm, the width to 4mm, and secure the stitches at the beginning and end of each seam. Computerised machines make these adjustments automatically and have an auto backtack.

HOW TO REVERSE APPLIQUÉ USING DOMINO STITCH

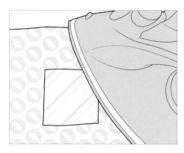

1 Cut a patch of appliqué fabric that is at least 25mm (1in) bigger than the appliqué design. Place the main fabric face up onto the appliqué fabric. Iron to hold in place.

2 Install the satin stitch or open toe foot on the machine and select the domino stitch.

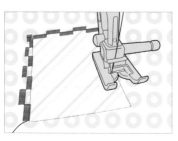

3 Stitch all the way around the appliqué, making sure that you backtack at the beginning and end.

 EXPERT TIP Satin stitches use a lot of thread so always double check that you have enough bobbin thread before you start.

ESSENTIAL FACTS

Also known as
Chequerboard stitch

Key feature
Block satin stitch that moves from side to side

Substitute stitch
Zigzag

Common uses
Decorative topstitch and appliqué

Presser foot
Satin stitch or open toe

Fabric type
All

Thread type
Polyester, cotton or embroidery

Needle type
Universal or embroidery

▶ SEE ALSO
Satin stitch foot, page 158

Decorative Stitches

Most computerised machines offer a variety of open decorative stitches such as botanical and graphic shapes, or motifs such as hearts, cars or animals. Computerised machines automatically adjust the length and width and have an auto backtack.

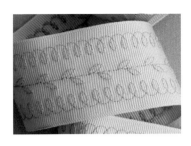

HOW TO MAKE FANCY TRIMS USING A DECORATIVE STITCH

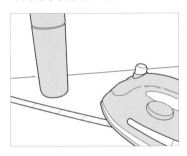

1 Mist the satin ribbon with spray starch and iron dry. Repeat several times so that the ribbon is very stiff. Mark a guide line for the stitch on the ribbon with a fabric marker or tailor's chalk.

2 Select the decorative stitch you want, insert a Microtex needle and thread the machine with the desired thread.

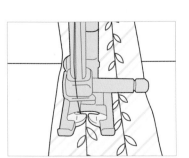

3 Stitch on the line. Repeat for additional rows as desired.

EXPERT TIP Decorative and embroidery stitches are not the same. Embroidery stitching is done by an embroidery machine with a hoop while decorative stitches are ones you can sew out just like a regular stitch.

ESSENTIAL FACTS

Also known as
Fancy stitch

Key feature
Repeating motif

Substitute stitch
Zigzag

Common uses
Decorative topstitch

Presser foot
Satin stitch or open toe

Fabric type
All

Thread type
Polyester, cotton or embroidery

Needle type
Universal, Microtex or embroidery

▶ SEE ALSO
Satin stitch foot, page 158

2

Hand Stitches

All sewing used to be done by hand until the invention of the sewing machine. And while machine sewing is certainly fast, there is something meditative and soothing about hand stitching. It is often preferable to machine sewing for certain techniques and fabrics. In this section we'll discuss how to create each stitch and indicate the ideal threads and needles to use with each stitch.

Backtack

The backtack secures a hand-stitched seam at the beginning and end to keep the stitches from coming undone. It is simply a double backstitch with the stitches on top of each other and is used instead of hand knotting the end of the thread. It can be used with any hand stitch and is used when stitching seams or hems, installing zippers and topstitching.

ESSENTIAL FACTS

Also known as
Securing stitch

Key feature
Double backstitch

Substitute stitch
Hand-tied knot

Common uses
Beginning and end of any seam

Fabric type
All

Thread type
All

Needle type
All

▶ SEE ALSO
Hand needles, page 146

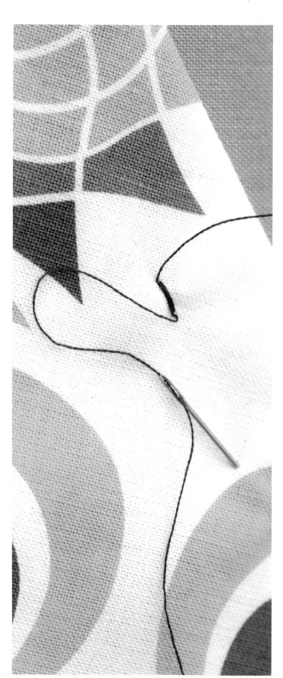

HOW TO SECURE A SEAM USING A BACKTACK

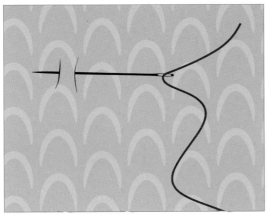

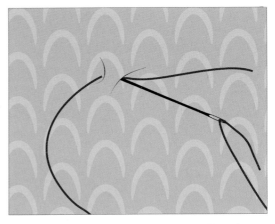

1 Cut a length of thread and thread the needle. Take a first stitch at the beginning of the seam, working from the top.

2 Bring the needle back up and take a small stitch back, about 3mm (1/8in) long.

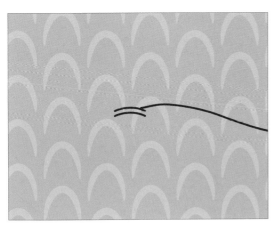

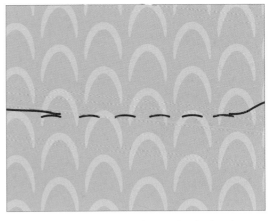

3 Bring the needle back up at the beginning spot and take another stitch back in the same spot. Stitch the remainder of the seam with the desired stitch.

4 At the end of the seam make another backtack to secure.

 EXPERT TIP If using polyester thread, don't lick it when threading the needle as polyester repels moisture. Instead, cut the end of the thread at an angle to make it easier to thread.

Backstitch

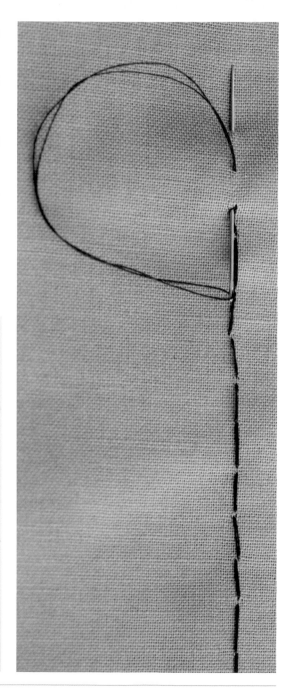

Backstitch is an all-purpose hand stitch for which the individual stitches are made in the opposite direction of the sewing. The hand version of a machine-sewn straight stitch, it is used for strong permanent seams. On the right side there is a continuous line of stitches while on the reverse the stitches overlap. Use this stitch for seams on garments, home décor items, accessories and soft toys. It can also be used for topstitching hems and attaching pockets and trims. Use a matching thread colour for seams and a small sharp needle. Backstitch can also be used with heavier threads and needles when topstitching.

ESSENTIAL FACTS

Also known as
Locking stitch

Key feature
Straight stitches in a row

Substitute stitch
Running stitch or machine-sewn straight stitch

Common uses
Seams, hems, darts and zippers

Fabric type
All

Thread type
Cotton, polyester, silk, topstitch or embroidery

Needle type
Betweens, sharps or embroidery

▶ SEE ALSO
Backtack, page 108

HOW TO STITCH A SEAM USING BACKSTITCH

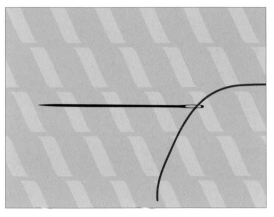

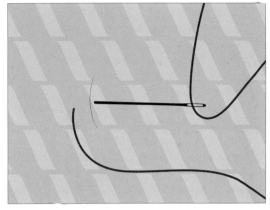

1 Pin fabrics together, right sides facing. Thread the needle and secure thread on wrong side by knotting it or backtacking. Bring the needle up at the start of the seam line.

2 Insert the needle into the fabric one stitch length to the right.

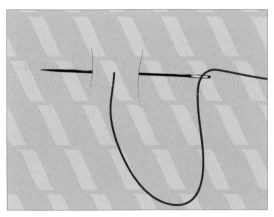

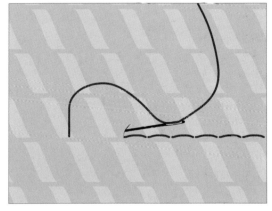

3 Bring the needle back up to the left of the initial needle entry point so that the total stitch length is 3mm ($1/8$in).

4 Insert the needle back into the fabric to the left of the end of the previous stitch and back up to the left, two stitch lengths along. Repeat for the length of the seam. At the end of the seam, backtack to secure.

 EXPERT TIP To keep long lengths of thread from tangling when handsewing, first coat them with beeswax or a silicone thread conditioner.

Running Stitch

The running stitch is a basic hand stitch used to connect fabric layers. The stitch is made by passing the needle in and out of the fabric in one direction. Small stitches, about 3mm (1/8in) long, are stronger than longer stitches. Use this stitch for seams, topstitching hems, attaching pockets and trims and hand quilting. Running stitch is not as strong as backstitch and so it should not be used on high-stress seams. Use a matching thread colour for seams and a small sharp needle. When topstitching, running stitch can also be used with heavier threads and needles.

ESSENTIAL FACTS

Also known as
Straight stitch

Key feature
Straight stitches in a row with a small space in between

Substitute stitch
Backstitch or machine-sewn straight stitch

Common uses
Seams, hems and topstitching

Fabric type
All

Thread type
Cotton, polyester, silk or hand quilting

Needle type
Betweens or sharps

▶ SEE ALSO
Backstitch, page 110

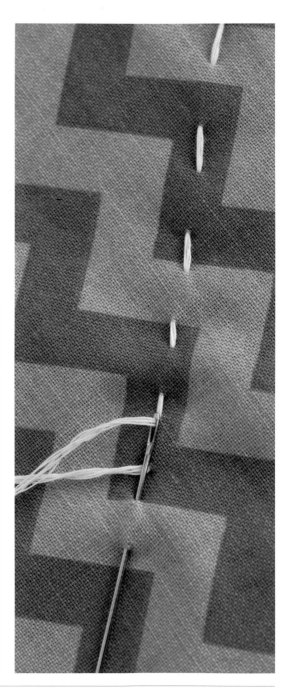

HOW TO STITCH A SEAM USING RUNNING STITCH

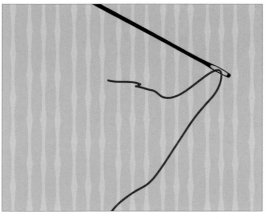

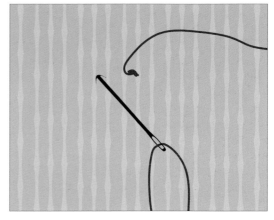

1 Pin fabrics together, right sides facing. Thread the needle and secure thread on wrong side by knotting it or backtacking. Bring the needle up at the start of the seam line.

2 Insert the needle back down into the fabric to the left of the needle entry point.

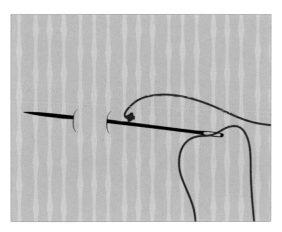

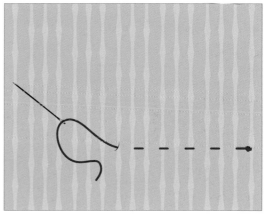

3 Bring the needle up to the left of the previous stitch.

4 Repeat for the length of the seam. At the end of the seam, backtack to secure.

 EXPERT TIP Saddle stitch is a variation of the running stitch using heavier thread and a smaller gap between the stitches. Use this on the edges of collars and cuffs.

Tacking Stitch

A variation of the running stitch, the tacking stitch has longer stitches, at least 13mm (1/2in) long. It is used to hold fabrics together prior to permanent machine or hand stitching. As pins can distort fabric, it is best to hand tack in a contrast colour before stitching. The stitches are easier to remove than machine tacking stitches. Hand tacking is commonly used to hold zippers, pockets and trims in place. It can be used when matching stripes and plaids, and to gather fabric. After the permanent stitch is sewn, the tacking stitches are removed.

ESSENTIAL FACTS

Also known as
Tack stitch and basting stitch

Key feature
Long straight stitches in a row

Substitute stitch
Running stitch or machine tacking stitch

Common uses
Hold fabrics together temporarily

Fabric type
All

Thread type
Cotton or silk

Needle type
Betweens or sharps

▶ SEE ALSO
Running stitch, page 112;
Machine tacking stitch, page 16

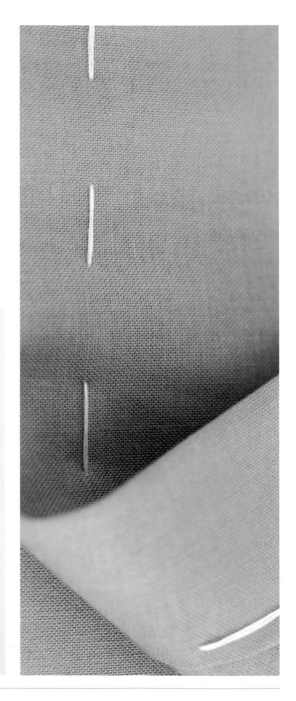

HOW TO TACK A SEAM USING TACKING STITCH

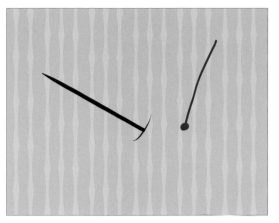

1 Pin fabrics together, right sides facing. Thread the needle and knot the end of the thread. Insert the needle at the beginning of the seam line and bring it back up to the left.

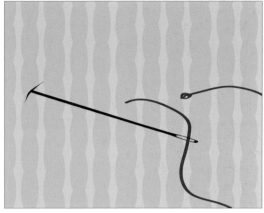

2 Insert the needle back down into the fabric to the left.

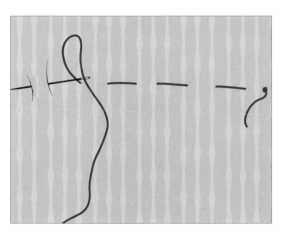

3 Repeat for the length of the seam, keeping the stitches evenly spaced. Backtack at the end.

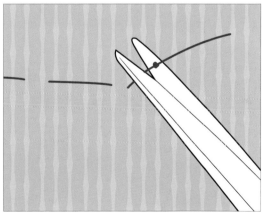

4 Remove the tacking stitches by cutting the knot and then either pulling the thread out or using a seam ripper.

 EXPERT TIP Use silk thread for tacking, as this pulls out easily. You can also use cotton thread, which breaks easily.

Blanket Stitch and Buttonhole Stitch

The blanket and buttonhole stitch are sewn in exactly the same way but the stitches are spaced much closer together for the buttonhole stitch. They finish a raw edge neatly and prevent fabric edges from ravelling. Stitch them with all-purpose polyester or cotton thread, or use contrasting topstitch, embroidery or metallic threads for a design element. Use the blanket stitch to finish edges on blankets, table cloths or napkins; use the buttonhole stitch to hand-stitch buttonholes for a couture touch. Use both to stitch appliqués.

ESSENTIAL FACTS

Also known as
Appliqué stitch

Key feature
L-shaped stitches along an edge

Substitute stitch
Whipstitch or overcast stitch

Common uses
Finish raw edges, buttonholes and appliqué

Fabric type
All

Thread type
All

Needle type
Betweens, sharps or embroidery

▶ SEE ALSO
Appliqué stitch, page 84

HOW TO FINISH AN EDGE USING BLANKET STITCH

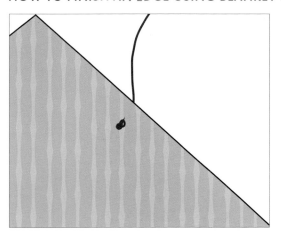

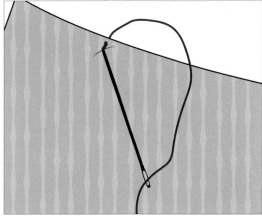

1 Cut a length of thread and thread the needle. Secure the thread on the wrong side near the fabric edge by either backtacking or knotting the thread.

2 Bring the needle to the front of the fabric by going over the fabric edge and insert the needle back into the fabric 13mm (1/2in) away from the fabric edge, working from back to front.

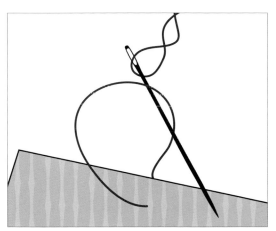

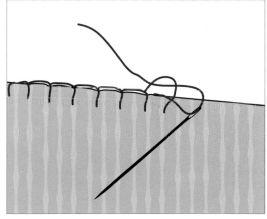

3 Loop the needle under the thread and then pull the thread taut.

4 Repeat for the length of the edge. At the end of the seam, backtack to secure.

 EXPERT TIP To keep your hand stitching straight, mark a guide line on the fabric with tailor's chalk or a fabric marker.

Overcast Stitch

The overcast stitch is used to neaten a raw edge to prevent fabrics from fraying and is designed to finish seam allowances. It is a stitch that loops over the fabric edge and the stitches are diagonal. Unlike the blanket and buttonhole stitch, however, the stitches do not loop under each other.
On fabrics that fray badly, be sure to space the stitches close together. Overcast stitch should be stitched with all-purpose polyester or cotton thread in a matching thread colour.

ESSENTIAL FACTS

Also known as
Overedge stitch

Key feature
Stitches wrapping over an edge

Substitute stitch
Blanket stitch or machine overcast stitch

Common uses
Finish raw edges to prevent fraying

Fabric type
All

Thread type
Polyester or cotton

Needle type
Betweens or sharps

▶ SEE ALSO
Blanket stitch, page 116

HOW TO FINISH AN EDGE USING OVERCAST STITCH

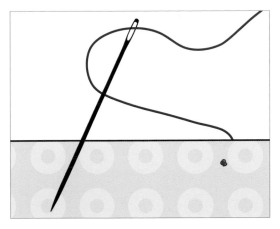

1 Cut a length of thread and thread the needle. Secure the thread on the wrong side near the fabric edge by either backtacking or knotting the thread.

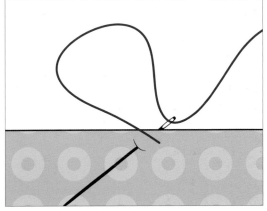

2 Bring the needle to the front of the fabric by going over the fabric edge and insert the needle back into the fabric 6mm (¹/₄in) away from the fabric edge, working from back to front.

3 Pull the thread taut but not so tightly that the fabric edge curls.

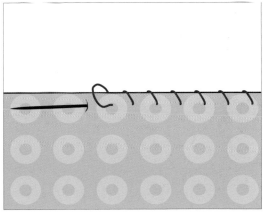

4 Bring the needle back up to the front, a stitch length away from the original stitch. Repeat steps until the edge is finished. At the end of the seam, backtack to secure.

 EXPERT TIP Very long threads tend to tangle easily. Work with a strand that is no longer than 60cm (24in) long.

Whipstitch

The whipstitch is very similar to the overcast stitch except it is used on a seam or to close an opening. It can also be used to hem a rolled edge and is commonly seen on silk scarves. The stitch loops over the fabric edge and the stitches move diagonally along the edge. Ideally it should be stitched with cotton, polyester or silk thread in a matching colour so that stitches are inconspicuous.

ESSENTIAL FACTS

Also known as
Rolled hem stitch

Key feature
Stitches wrapping over an edge

Substitute stitch
Blanket stitch

Common uses
Rolled hems and to close openings

Fabric type
All

Thread type
Polyester, cotton or silk

Needle type
Betweens or sharps

▶ SEE ALSO
Overcast stitch, page 118

HOW TO STITCH A ROLLED HEM USING WHIPSTITCH

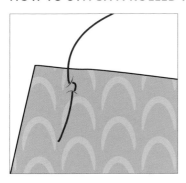

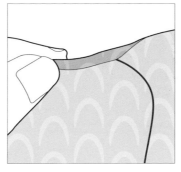

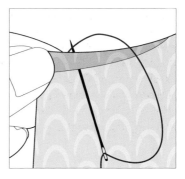

1 Thread the needle and hold the fabric with the wrong side facing you. Secure the thread on the wrong side near the fabric edge by either backtacking or knotting the thread. The knot will later be concealed in the rolled edge.

2 Roll the fabric towards you so it is turned under 3mm (1/8in) twice, concealing the raw edge and the thread knot.

3 Bring the needle to the top of the fabric by going over the rolled fabric edge, down through the fabric, and out of the fabric next to the fold.

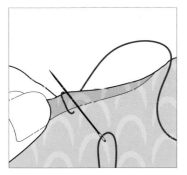

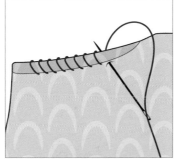

4 Working left to right, take another stitch over the edge, again going back down through the single layer next to the fold.

5 Continue rolling and whipping until the edge is finished. At the end of the seam, backtack through the hem to secure and hide the thread tail in the hem.

 EXPERT TIP If the fabric is very slippery, spray starch the edge to make it easier to work with. Always test spray starch on a scrap to ensure it doesn't stain the fabric.

Blind Hem Stitch

The blind hem stitch is an invisible stitch used to hem garments and curtains. It is the hand version of the machine blind hem stitch. The stitches are barely noticeable on the right side and there is a V-shaped stitch hidden in the hem fold on the wrong side of the fabric. The hem is folded under twice so it is best to use on straight edges. The stitch has a bit of give but it is not quite as strong as a topstitched hem. It should be stitched with cotton, polyester or silk in a matching thread colour to keep the stitches as inconspicuous as possible on the right side.

ESSENTIAL FACTS

Also known as
Invisible hem

Key feature
Nearly invisible stitches on the right side

Substitute stitch
Slip stitch

Common uses
Hems on garments and drapes

Fabric type
All

Thread type
Polyester, cotton or silk

Needle type
Betweens or sharps for garments; darners for curtains

▶ SEE ALSO
Straight blind hem stitch, page 30

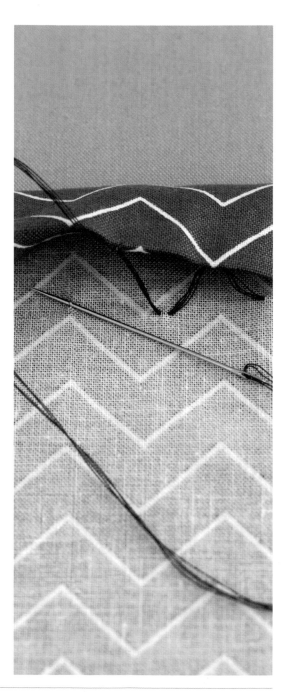

HOW TO HEM USING BLIND HEM STITCH

1 Press the hem under the full amount of the hem allowance. Press the raw edge under 6mm (¼in). Pin.

2 Cut a length of thread, thread the needle, and knot the thread. Working with the wrong side of the fabric facing you, secure the thread in the hem fold. The knot will be concealed in the hem.

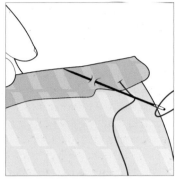

3 Take a tiny stitch through the fabric, catching just a couple of the threads of the fabric just below where the hem fold meets the fabric.

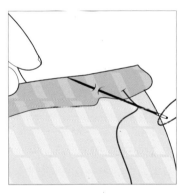

4 Insert the needle through the inside fold of the hem and take a small stitch to the left, making sure you only catch the fold.

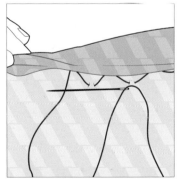

5 Working right to left, continue stitching one stitch into the garment and one into the hem until the hem is finished. At the end, secure the thread and hide the thread tail by backtacking through the hem.

 EXPERT TIP Press the hem lightly at the end to ensure that a ridge from the fold does not show through on the right side.

Slip Stitch

The slip stitch is an invisible stitch used to attach one fabric to another and is used for hemming, to attach linings, and to attach appliqués, trims and pockets. It can also be used to close openings on pillows and linings. It is often used to finish bindings on quilts. Although it shouldn't show on either the right or wrong side, always make sure you match your thread colour to the fabric in case any stitches do show. Use small stitches in order to avoid leaving any gaps in the seam.

ESSENTIAL FACTS

Also known as
Slip hem

Key feature
Nearly invisible stitches on the right side

Substitute stitch
Ladder stitch

Common uses
Hems, bindings, pockets, trims and to close openings

Fabric type
Wovens

Thread type
Polyester or cotton

Needle type
Betweens or sharps for garments; darners for curtains

▶ SEE ALSO
Straight stitch, page 10

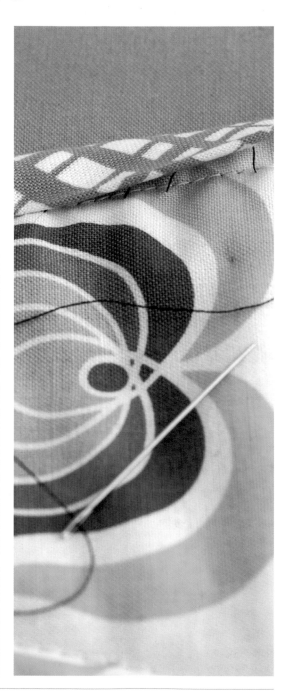

HOW TO FINISH A BINDING USING SLIP STITCH

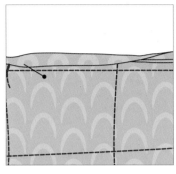

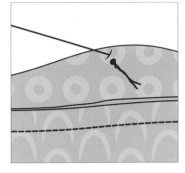

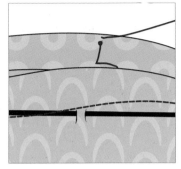

1 Stitch the binding to the right side of the quilt using either a machine straight stitch or a hand backstitch. Fold the bias binding over to the back side of the quilt and pin.

2 Cut a length of thread, thread the needle and knot the thread. Secure the thread in the bottom layer of the bias binding. The knot will be concealed in the fold.

3 Take a tiny stitch through the quilt, catching just a couple of the threads of the fabric just above where the bias binding folds to meet the quilt.

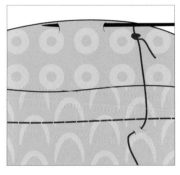

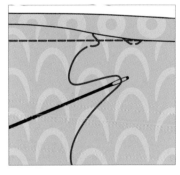

4 Insert the needle through the edge of the bias binding and slide the needle through the fold 4 to 5 stitch lengths. Take a tiny stitch through the quilt, again only catching a couple of threads.

5 Working right to left, continue stitching one stitch into the quilt and then sliding through the binding until you reach the end. Backtack through the binding to secure and hide the thread tail.

 EXPERT TIP When stitching through heavy fabrics, a thimble can save your fingers from painful pressure and needle pokes. Thimbles can be made of metal, leather, rubber or plastic. Whichever type you choose, it's important for a thimble to fit comfortably and stay in place.

Ladder Stitch

The ladder stitch is an invisible stitch that joins an opening in a seam. It is sewn from the right side when you cannot work from the reverse side, and is commonly used to close up openings on pillows, cushions and soft toys. It can also be used to finish openings left on linings and to repair torn seams. When using the ladder stitch, it is imperative to match your thread colour well in case your stitches show. You should also use small stitches in order to avoid leaving any gaps in the seam.

ESSENTIAL FACTS

Also known as
Invisible stitch

Key feature
Invisible joining stitch

Substitute stitch
Slip stitch

Common uses
To close openings on pillows and linings and for repairs

Fabric type
All woven fabrics; not used on knits

Thread type
Cotton or polyester

Needle type
Betweens or sharps

▶ SEE ALSO
Backtack stitch, page 108

HOW TO CLOSE AN OPENING USING LADDER STITCH

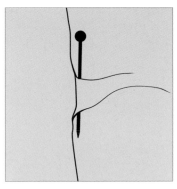 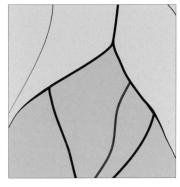 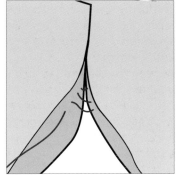

1 Pin the opening closed to keep your hands free for sewing. Cut a length of thread, thread the needle, and knot one thread end. Take a first stitch at one end of the opening, hiding the thread tail just inside the fold.

2 Then take the next stitch in the opposite fold, catching the fabric, again just inside the fold, and pull the thread taut.

3 Take the next stitch straight across from that last stitch, again catching just the inside the fold. Continue stitching in this pattern until the seam is closed.

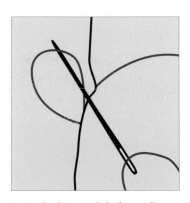 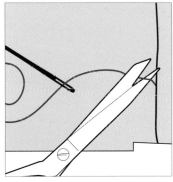

4 On the last stitch, before pulling the thread completely taut, pull the needle through the loop to make a self-knot to secure the stitches. Repeat to make a double knot.

5 To hide the thread tails, stitch the needle back in the seam and pull through to an inconspicuous spot and then pull tight. Clip the thread, and the thread tail will be hidden inside the project.

 EXPERT TIP You can also use a backtack stitch at the beginning to secure the thread tails. Make sure the backtack stitch is hidden in the seam.

Darning Stitch

The darning stitch is used to repair holes or worn areas in woven fabrics. Threads are stitched in one direction across the hole as a base, then threads are woven through base threads at a 90-degree angle to mimic the weave of the fabric. Match your thread colour and weight as closely as you can to the base fabric in order to make the repair as discreet as possible. Use a standard embroidery hoop to keep the fabric taut and prevent it from bunching. For large holes you may need to apply a backing fabric for strength.

ESSENTIAL FACTS

Also known as
Repair stitch

Key feature
Rows of stitches woven in perpendicular directions

Substitute stitch
Machine darning

Common uses
Mending holes or worn fabrics

Fabric type
All woven fabrics; not used on knits

Thread type
Cotton or polyester

Needle type
Betweens, sharps or darners

▶ SEE ALSO
Machine darning stitch, page 70

HOW TO MEND A HOLE USING DARNING STITCH

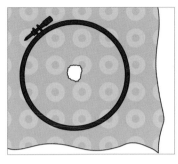

1 Hoop the fabric in an embroidery hoop. Keep the area to repair in the centre of the hoop.

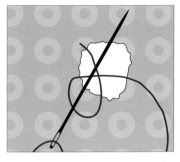

2 Cut a length of thread, thread the needle and knot one thread end. Take a first stitch going from the top left to the bottom left of the hole. Before you pull the thread completely taut, pull the needle through the loop to make a self-knot to secure the stitches.

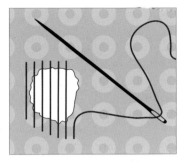

3 Stitch back up across the hole one stitch length to the right. To secure, knot the thread with a loop. Continue stitching across the hole in this manner until you have covered the hole. Knot the thread or backtack at the end.

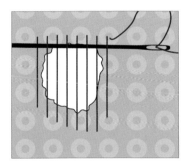

4 Cut another length of thread, thread it, and knot one thread end. Take a stitch from the top right to the top left of the hole, weaving over and under the vertical threads. Before you pull the thread taut, pull the needle through the loop to make a self-knot to secure the stitches.

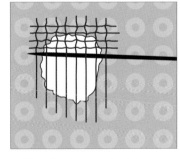

5 Stitch back across the hole a stitch length down. Weave the needle in the same way but start by going under rather than over the thread. Continue across the hole in this way, alternating starting over or under the thread. At the end, knot the thread or backtack

 EXPERT TIP Make sure you anchor the stitches far enough from the hole that the stitches don't come loose.

French Tack

The French tack is a chain made by stitching buttonhole stitches over a few strands of thread to loosely join two fabrics together. It is often used to hold linings to coats, jackets and skirts at the hem or to attach curtain linings to the main curtain panel at the hem. It allows the fabrics to still hang independently of each other and move freely, and prevents fabric strain. Use a strong thread such as polyester or silk because cotton thread may break under strain.

ESSENTIAL FACTS

Also known as
Swing tack

Key feature
Thread chain

Substitute stitch
None

Common uses
To attach linings loosely to main fabrics at hems

Fabric type
All

Thread type
Polyester or silk

Needle type
Betweens, sharps or darners

▶ SEE ALSO
Blanket stitch and buttonhole stitch, page 116

HOW TO STITCH A FRENCH TACK

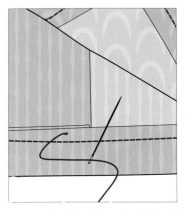

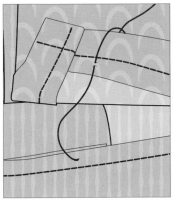

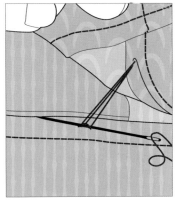

1 Cut a length of thread and thread the needle. Fold back the hem of the lining fabric and secure the thread into the main fabric by taking a couple of backtacks.

2 Take a first stitch into the lining fabric by catching just a couple of threads of the lining.

3 Take a stitch back through the main fabric, keeping the two fabrics apart so that the stitch is loose. Go back and forth between the two fabrics three more times.

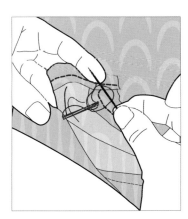

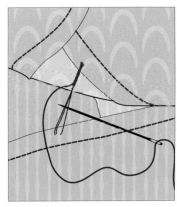

4 Now start wrapping the thread around the strands using a buttonhole stitch.

5 Continue until the whole bar is covered with buttonhole stitches. Backtack to secure.

 EXPERT TIP You cannot use a machine to replicate this stitch, as it is a couture technique and must be sewn by hand.

Bartack

The bartack is a thread bar designed to reinforce points of strain such as pocket corners, tops of pleats or skirt vents. Similar to the French tack, it is a thread chain made by stitching buttonhole stitches over a few strands of thread. However, it is stitched on the surface of a fabric. Use a strong thread such as polyester or silk because cotton may break under strain. You can match the thread colour to conceal the stitches or use a contrasting colour to make the bartacks a design detail, such as on jeans.

ESSENTIAL FACTS

Also known as
Tack

Key feature
Thread chain

Substitute stitch
Machine-stitched bartack

Common uses
Reinforce points of strain

Fabric type
All

Thread type
Polyester, silk or topstitch

Needle type
Sharps, darners or embroidery

▶ SEE ALSO
Blanket stitch and buttonhole stitch, page 116

HOW TO STITCH A BARTACK

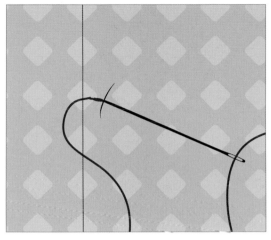

1 Cut a length of thread and thread the needle. Take a stitch into the fabric at the desired position for the bartack and backtack to secure the thread.

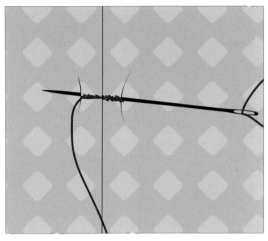

2 Take three to four long stitches through all the layers of fabric.

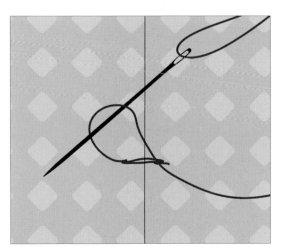

3 Now start wrapping the thread around the strands using a buttonhole stitch.

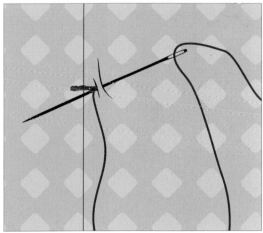

4 Continue until the whole bar is covered with buttonhole stitches. Backtack to secure.

 EXPERT TIP Bartacks can also be stitched at the fabric edges and used as loops for buttons.

Tailor's Tack

A tailor's tack is a temporary stitch to mark points of reference on fabric. It is loosely stitched through layers of fabric and cut so that tufts of thread are left behind. Tailor's tacks mark pocket placement, button and buttonhole locations, zipper stops, darts and pleats. They are used on fine fabrics when fabric marker or chalk marks cannot be safely removed. They can be stitched through the tissue pattern pieces onto the fabric; the tissues can be pulled away when the threads are cut. After sewing the permanent stitch, tailor's tacks are removed.

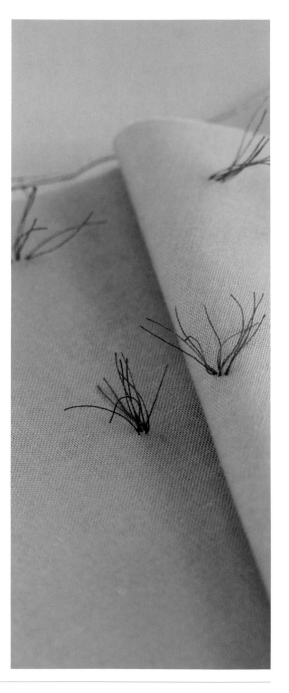

ESSENTIAL FACTS

Also known as
Tack stitch

Key feature
Little tufts of thread

Substitute stitch
Tacking stitch

Common uses
Mark reference points on fabric

Fabric type
All

Thread type
Cotton or silk

Needle type
Betweens or sharps

▶ SEE ALSO
Tacking stitch, page 114

HOW TO STITCH TAILOR'S TACKS

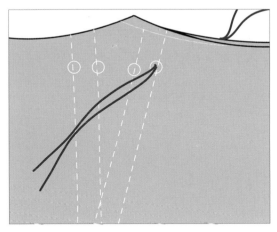

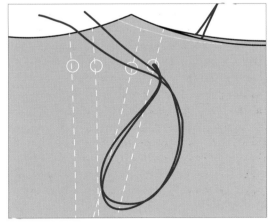

1 Thread the needle with a double strand of thread. Do not knot the thread. Take a small stitch through the pattern paper and both fabric layers. Leave a 7.5cm (3in) thread tail.

2 Take another small stitch on top of the first one. Do not pull the thread through all the way. Leave a loop about 5–7.5cm (2–3in) long.

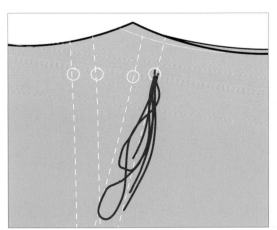

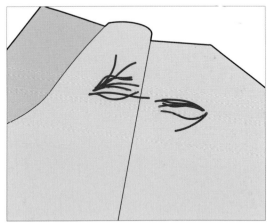

3 Take another stitch and leave a big loop. Cut the thread, leaving a 7.5cm (3in) thread tail.

4 Remove the pattern and pull the layers of fabric apart. Clip the threads in the middle, leaving tufts of thread on each layer.

 EXPERT TIP A contrasting thread colour makes the tailor's tacks easier to see and remove.

Diagonal Tacking

The diagonal tacking stitch has long diagonal floats of thread on the top of the fabric and horizontal floats on the bottom. It is used across the fabric surface to hold layers of fabric together. It keeps slippery fabrics from shifting during the construction process or helps hold non-fusible interfacing in place. It can also be used to hold pockets, waistbands, pleats and gathers in place before they are stitched down. Diagonal tacking stitches can be removed after the permanent stitch is sewn. Use silk or cotton thread for diagonal tacking.

ESSENTIAL FACTS

Also known as
Diagonal basting

Key feature
Long diagonal stitches on top, horizontal stitches on the reverse

Substitute stitch
Tacking stitch or machine tacking stitch

Common uses
Hold fabrics together temporarily

Fabric type
All

Thread type
Cotton or silk

Needle type
Betweens or sharps

▶ SEE ALSO
Machine tacking stitch, page 16;
Tacking stitch, page 114

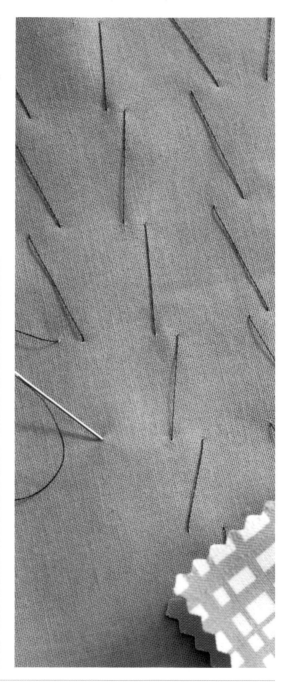

HOW TO TACK USING DIAGONAL TACKING STITCH

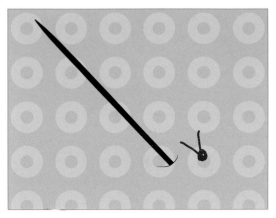

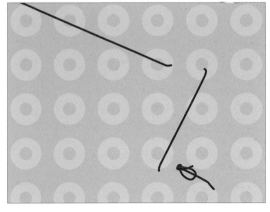

1 Cut a length of thread and thread the needle. Knot the end of the thread. Working from bottom to top, take a small horizontal stitch to the left through both fabric layers.

2 Take a diagonal stitch above and to the right of the previous stitch and then another horizontal stitch to the left.

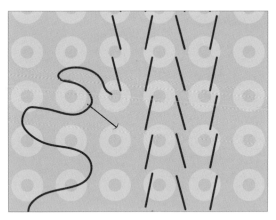

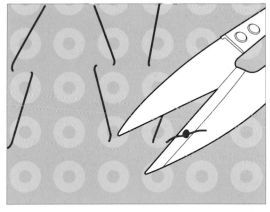

3 Continue stitching the line of stitches in this manner until complete. Stitch another row mirroring the first row. Continue stitching rows of stitching until you have filled the fabric area.

4 Remove the tacking stitches when they are no longer needed by cutting the knot and then either pulling out the thread or using a seam ripper.

 EXPERT TIP Don't press fine fabrics while the tacking stitches are in place as the tacking thread can leave permanent impressions in the fabric.

Pad Stitch

The pad stitch looks like the diagonal tacking stitch with long diagonal floats of thread on the top of the fabric. But pad stitching only catches a thread of the main fabric and the floats are on the wrong side. It is a tailoring technique used to permanently hold layers of fabric and interfacing together and add firmness. It can also be used to impose a curve or roll to the layers. It is used on men's suit jackets on the lapels and under the collar to give the structure and roll line. Use a strong thread such as silk and ensure it matches your main fabric.

ESSENTIAL FACTS

Also known as
Tailor stitching

Key feature
Long diagonal stitches on the wrong side; nearly invisible stitches on the face side

Substitute stitch
None

Common uses
In tailoring, to hold fabrics together permanently, add firmness and add curvature

Fabric type
Suiting

Thread type
Silk

Needle type
Betweens or sharps

▶ SEE ALSO
Diagonal tacking, page 136

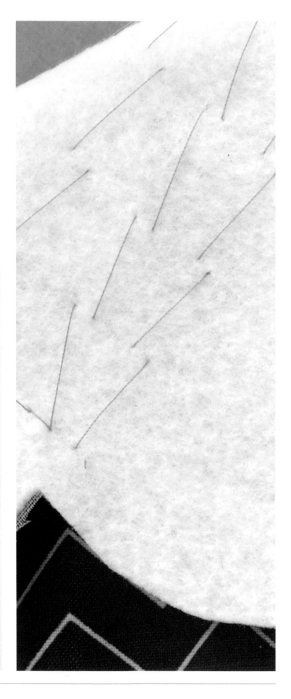

HOW TO APPLY INTERFACING USING PAD STITCH

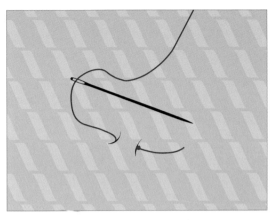

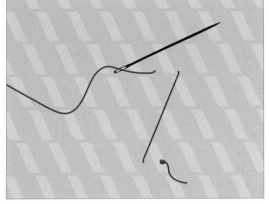

1 Thread the needle. Knot the end of the thread. Working from the wrong side, take a tiny horizontal stitch left through both fabric layers, just catching a thread of the fashion fabric on the bottom layer.

2 Take a diagonal stitch above and to the right of the previous stitch and then another tiny horizontal stitch to the left.

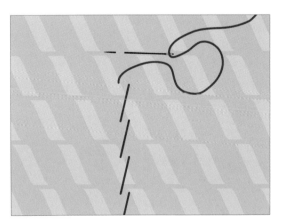

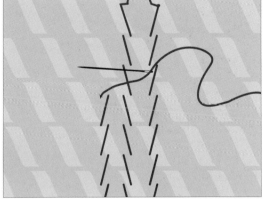

3 Continue stitching in this manner until complete.

4 Stitch another row mirroring the first row. Continue making rows of stitching until you have filled the fabric area. Use smaller and denser stitches in areas that need more firmness.

 EXPERT TIP Like the French tack, there is no substitute machine stitch for this. It is a sign of quality tailoring.

Prick Stitch

The prick stitch is a strong permanent stitch very similar to the basic backstitch but the surface stitch is tiny, with a longer stitch on the wrong side. It is used to stitch edges on tailored coats and suits and to secure facings and linings to prevent them from rolling. It is also used to hand stitch a zipper into a couture garment. The prick stitch can also be used for topstitching hems and attaching pockets and trims. Make sure the colour of your thread matches the fabric as closely as possible and use a small, sharp needle.

ESSENTIAL FACTS

Also known as
Pick stitch

Key feature
Tiny straight stitches in a row

Substitute stitch
Backstitch or machine-sewn straight stitch

Common uses
Topstitching, hems and zippers

Fabric type
Wovens

Thread type
Cotton or polyester

Needle type
Betweens or sharps

▶ SEE ALSO
Backstitch, page 110

HOW TO STITCH A SEAM USING PRICK STITCH

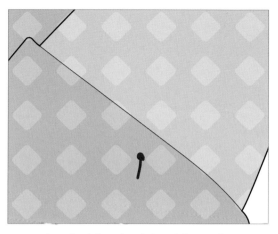

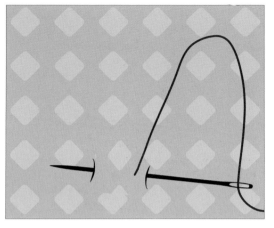

1 Cut a length of thread and thread the needle. Secure the thread on the wrong side by either backtacking or knotting the thread. Bring the needle to the front at the beginning of the seam line.

2 Take a tiny stitch to the right and bring the needle back up a stitch length to the left.

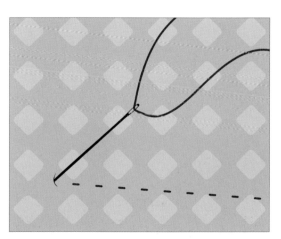

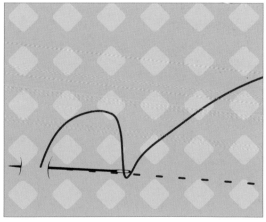

3 Take another tiny backstitch to the right and bring the needle back up a stitch length to the left. The stitches should look like tiny dots.

4 Repeat for the length of the seam. At the end of the seam, backtack to secure.

 EXPERT TIP If your thread tangles while stitching, let the needle dangle and the thread will untwist.

Catch Stitch

The catch stitch is an invisible hem stitch used to hem garments and curtains. It is the hand version of the machine stretch blind hem stitch. The catch stitch is flexible and can be used to hem stretch wovens and knits. It can also be used to attach the raw edges of a facing to the inside of a garment. The stitches are barely noticeable on the right side and create cross-shaped stitches on the wrong side of the fabric. Catch stitch should be stitched with cotton or polyester thread in a matching thread colour to keep the stitches as inconspicuous as possible on the right side.

ESSENTIAL FACTS

Also known as
Herringbone stitch

Key feature
Nearly invisible stitches on the right side, cross-stitches on the wrong side

Substitute stitch
Blind hem stitch

Common uses
Hems on garments

Fabric type
Stretch fabrics

Thread type
Polyester or cotton

Needle type
Betweens and sharps for garments, darners for curtains

▶ SEE ALSO
Stretch blind hem stitch, page 32;
Blind hem stitch, page 122

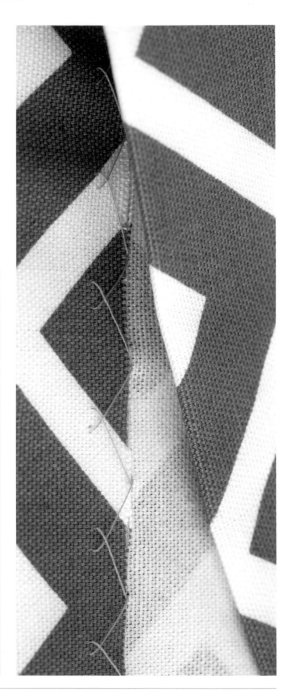

HOW TO HEM USING CATCH STITCH

1 Press under the full amount of the hem allowance. Pin.

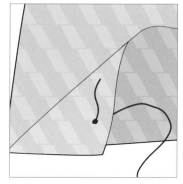

2 Cut a length of thread, thread the needle, and knot the thread. Working with the wrong side of the fabric facing you, secure the thread in the hem fold. The knot will be concealed in the hem.

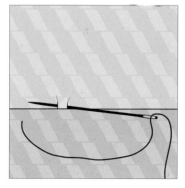

3 Working left to right, take a tiny stitch through the fabric, catching only a couple of the threads of the fabric just above where the hem fold meets the fabric.

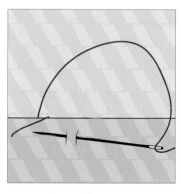

4 Insert the needle diagonally through the hem and take a small stitch, making sure to only catch the fold.

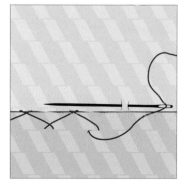

5 Continue stitching one stitch into the garment and one into the hem until the hem is finished. At the end of the hem, backtack through the hem to secure and hide the thread tail in the hem.

 EXPERT TIP Take frequent breaks when doing a lot of hand stitching. At least once an hour, let your eyes and fingers rest for five minutes and then resume the project.

3

Tools and Equipment

There are many different types of thread available for machine and hand stitching. How do you know which to use? Which needle type is best for the task at hand? This section reviews needles, threads and common presser feet as well as how to work with mechanical, computerised and vintage sewing machines.

Hand Needles

Handsewing needles have an eye at the top and then taper to a point at the other end. The needle width, length, point shape and eye size are intended for different sewing tasks, fabric or thread. Handsewing needles are sized by number; thicker needles have lower numbers and finer needles have higher numbers. Always use a needle size that is thin enough to go through the fabric without damaging it but large enough not to bend. Make sure the eye size is large enough for the thread being used.

SHARPS

Key feature
Medium length, sharp point, round eye

Common uses
General purpose, used for most basic handsewing tasks

Sizes
1 to 12

Thread type
Cotton or polyester

Fabric type
Wovens

BETWEENS

Key feature
Short length, sharp point, round eye

Common uses
Detail work and hand quilting

Sizes
1 to 12

Thread type
Cotton and polyester

Fabric type
Wovens

DARNING

Key feature
Long length, sharp point, long eye

Common uses
Mending and darning holes

Sizes
1 to 9

Thread type
Cotton and polyester

Fabric type
All

EMBROIDERY

Key feature
Medium length, sharp point, extra-long eye to accommodate multiple strands of embroidery floss

Common uses
Hand embroidery using embroidery floss

Sizes
1 to 10

Thread type
Embroidery floss

Fabric type
Wovens

TAPESTRY

Key feature
Thick, large eye for thick threads and yarns and blunt point to go through fabric without creating a hole

Common uses
Needlepoint, cross-stitch, embroidery and decorative stitching on loosely woven fabrics; threading ribbons

Sizes
13 to 28

Thread type
Embroidery floss, ribbon or yarn

Fabric type
Needlepoint canvas, aida cloth, or open-mesh fabrics

CHENILLE

Key feature
Thick, large eye for yarn or ribbon, sharp point to easily go through stiff fabrics

Common uses
Decorative stitching and ribbon embroidery

Sizes
13 to 26

Thread type
Embroidery floss, ribbon or yarn

Fabric type
Canvas

YARN DARNING

Key feature
Very thick with extra-large eye

Common uses
Darning with thick yarns, decorative stitches and threading ribbons

Sizes
14 to 18

Thread type
Embroidery floss, ribbon or yarn

Fabric type
Needlepoint canvas, aida cloth or open-mesh fabrics

BEADING

Key feature
Long, very thin and flexible

Common uses
Stitch beads and sequins onto fabric

Sizes
10 to 15

Thread type
Cotton or polyester

Fabric type
All

 EXPERT TIP Needles come in packages of one type or size or in assortments. Specialty hand needles are frequently sold together in a booklet called repair needles.

CANVAS AND CARPET

Key feature
Medium length, sharp point, thick needle and an elongated eye

Common uses
Stitching very thick heavy fabrics such as canvas and carpets

Sizes
16 to 18

Thread type
Polyester or heavy threads like topstitch

Fabric type
Canvas, upholstery or carpets

LEATHER/GLOVER

Key feature
Triangular point that easily passes through leather without causing any damage

Common uses
Stitching on leather

Sizes
1 to 10

Thread type
Polyester

Fabric type
Leather, suede, vinyl, plastic or wovens

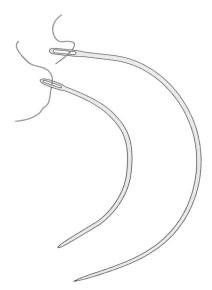

CURVED NEEDLE

Key feature
Curved with sharp point

Common uses
Allows access to hard-to-reach areas

Sizes
Lengths varying from 38mm (1½in) to 15cm (6in)

Thread type
Cotton, polyester or topstitch

Fabric type
Wovens

SACK

Key feature
Blunt point, thick needle and an extra-long eye

Common uses
Heavy-duty darning

Sizes
3 to 9

Thread type
Yarn or heavy threads like topstitch

Fabric type
Loosely woven fabrics such as burlap

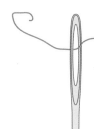

SAIL

Key feature
Triangular point, thick needle, long length and an elongated eye

Common uses
Stitching very heavy and stiff fabric with heavy threads

Sizes
1 to 5

Thread type
Heavy threads like topstitch

Fabric type
Heavy canvas or thick leather

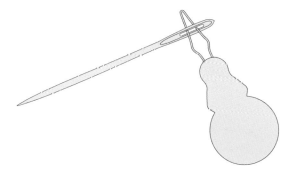

 EXPERT TIP Threading a needle is sometimes a challenge especially if your eyesight is less than perfect. A needle threader can make the task a lot easier. Simply insert the wire loop through the eye of the needle, drop the thread through the loop, and pull wire and thread through the needle eye.

Machine needles have the eye at the bottom near the point and a flat back at the top of the shank. The fronts of machine needles are grooved to cradle the thread as it penetrates the fabric. The indentation above the eye on the back of the needle is called the scarf and it helps the bobbin hook catch the needle thread. These needles have two numbers to indicate the size. The first number is the European number and it measures the diameter of the needle blade, while the second number is the corresponding American size. Low numbers indicate fine needles while higher numbers mean thicker needles.

UNIVERSAL NEEDLE

Key feature
Slightly rounded point

Common uses
General-purpose needle for most sewing tasks. Use for seams, buttonholes, tacking, hems, topstitching, zippers, overcasting, appliqué and sewing trims

Sizes
All sizes from 60/8 up to 120/19; 80/12 is most commonly used

Thread type
Cotton or polyester

Fabric type
Wovens

BALLPOINT/JERSEY NEEDLE

Key feature
Rounded point designed to slide between fibres rather than cutting through them, which can damage the fabric

Common uses
Seams, topstitching, hems, overcasting and buttonholes

Sizes
70/10, 80/12, 90/14 and 100/16

Thread type
Polyester

Fabric type
Knits

DENIM/JEANS NEEDLE

Key feature
Sharp point and strong blade to pierce through thick fabrics

Common uses
Seams, topstitching, overcasting, hems, buttonholes and zippers

Sizes
70/10, 80/12, 90/14, 100/16 and 110/18

Thread type
Polyester

Fabric type
Heavyweight or tightly woven fabrics

QUILTING NEEDLE

Key feature
Sharp point and tapered blade to easily penetrate multiple layers of lofty fabric

Common uses
Machine-quilting

Sizes
75/11, 80/12 and 90/14

Thread type
Cotton

Fabric type
Wovens

STRETCH NEEDLE

Key feature
Slightly rounded point and a deep scarf to help the needle thread catch the bobbin hook better than a ballpoint needle and prevent skipped stitches

Common uses
Seams, topstitching, hems, overcasting and buttonholes

Sizes
75/11 and 90/14

Thread type
Polyester

Fabric type
Lightweight knit fabrics or knits with spandex

MICROTEX NEEDLE

Key feature
Very thin, sharp point designed to easily pierce through thin and delicate fabrics

Common uses
Seams, topstitching, hems and piecing quilts – whenever precision is essential

Sizes
60/8, 70/10, 80/12, 90/14, 100/16 and 110/18

Thread type
Cotton or silk

Fabric type
Delicate fabrics

 EXPERT TIP Always keep extra needles on hand. It is Murphy's Law that you will break your last needle right before the last step of your project.

TOPSTITCH NEEDLE

Key feature
Sharp point, wide groove and elongated eye to accommodate thick topstitching thread

Common uses
Heirloom stitches

Sizes
80/12, 90/14 and 100/16

Thread type
Topstitch

Fabric type
Wovens

WING/HEMSTITCH NEEDLE

Key feature
Wing on each side of the needle

Common uses
Heirloom stitches

Sizes
100/16 and 120/19

Thread type
Cotton or decorative threads

Fabric type
Light to medium-weight wovens

LEATHER NEEDLE

Key feature
Sharp, wedge-shaped point to cut cleanly through non-woven materials without causing damage

Common uses
Seams and topstitching

Sizes
70/10, 80/12, 90/14, 100/16 and 110/18

Thread type
Polyester

Fabric type
Leather, plastic, vinyl and oilcloth

EMBROIDERY NEEDLE

Key feature
Slightly rounded point, enlarged eye and wide groove

Common uses
Decorative stitches

Sizes
75/11 and 90/14

Thread type
Rayon embroidery and decorative threads

Fabric type
All

EXPERT TIP Replace the needle every three or four projects, or eight hours of sewing time. Each time the needle makes a stitch, it dulls a bit. A dull needle causes skipped stitches, can damage your fabric, is prone to breaking and can cause thread jams.

METALLIC NEEDLE

Key feature
Slightly rounded point and elongated coated eye to prevent delicate threads from shredding

Common uses
Decorative stitches

Sizes
80/12 and 90/14

Thread type
Metallic

Fabric type
Wovens

TWIN NEEDLE

Key feature
Two needles attached to one shank: with universal, stretch, denim, metallic or embroidery needles

Common uses
Decorative stitching, pintucks, topstitching and hems

Sizes
Depends on type. First number: distance between needles; second: needle size

Thread type
All

Fabric type
All

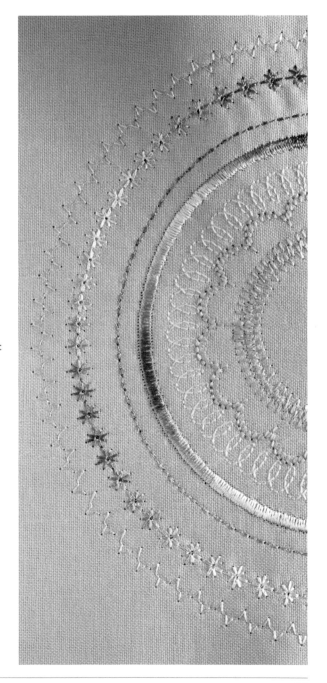

POLYESTER

This strong all-purpose thread can be used for machine and hand stitching. But polyester thread can be too strong for delicate fabrics. Polyester thread has slight elasticity and is the best choice for stretch-knit fabrics.

Key feature
Strong, colourfast, resists shrinkage and elastic

Common uses
General sewing

Fabric type
All except for delicates

Needle type
Universal, stretch, ballpoint, leather, Microtex or denim

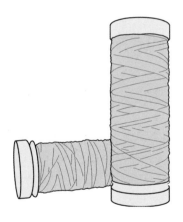

COTTON

Cotton thread can be used for machine and hand stitching. The stitches can be ironed at a high heat. Cotton is not as strong as polyester thread and is more susceptible to deterioration. Cotton thread does not stretch and should not be used for knit fabrics. Do not use it for leather; the tannins will wear through the thread.

Key feature
Can be ironed at high heat

Common uses
General sewing and quilting

Fabric type
Wovens

Needle type
Universal, Microtex or quilting

 EXPERT TIP When matching a thread colour, unwind a single strand of thread from the spool and lay it on the fabric. When deciding between two close colours, choose the darker colour because it will disappear into the fabric.

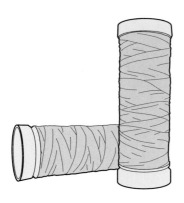

SILK

Silk thread is thinner than all-purpose cotton or polyester threads but is strong and has a lustrous shine. It's the best choice for hand and machine tacking because its smoothness makes the thread easy to remove. It is expensive and is often used for sewing on silk and other fine fabrics. When machine stitching with silk thread, make sure you use a fine needle, such as a Microtex sharp needle, and tighten the tension slightly to accommodate a thinner thread.

Key feature
Thin, strong and lustrous

Common uses
Tacking, decorative stitches and general sewing

Fabric type
Wovens

Needle type
Universal or Microtex

ELASTIC

Elastic thread is used for elastic shirring. It is used only in the bobbin and is hand wound onto it. Elastic thread is commonly available only in black or white, and polyester or cotton thread is used in the needle in any colour. As you stitch multiple rows of elastic shirring the fabric will gather up. To create more gathers, steam the completed rows to shrink the elastic thread and gather up the fabric even more. This thread can be used instead of smocking.

Key feature
Stretches

Common uses
Elastic shirring

Fabric type
Light to medium-weight wovens and knits

Needle type
Universal, stretch, ballpoint or Microtex

 EXPERT TIP Threads come in various thicknesses. A higher number indicates a thinner and finer thread. All-purpose thread is size 50.

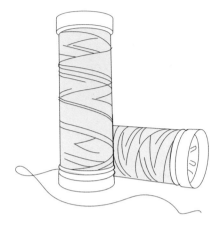

TOPSTITCH

Topstitch thread is a heavy, strong thread made of polyester. It is often used in a contrasting colour for topstitching seams and is also an excellent choice for hand stitching buttons. Lower the upper tension to accommodate the thick thread and use all-purpose thread in the bobbin. A topstitch needle is required because it has a large eye to accommodate the thick thread. Topstitch thread comes in a limited range of colours but you can mimic the look of topstitch thread by using two strands of all-purpose thread.

Key feature
Strong, colourfast, resists shrinkage and elastic

Common uses
Topstitch, buttons and faggoting

Fabric type
Wovens

Needle type
Topstitch for machine stitching, darners or embroidery for handstitching

HAND QUILTING

Hand-quilting thread is made from cotton and is used for hand stitching, for example, on quilts. It has a special glazed coating for added strength and smoothness and to prevent tangling. It should never be used for machine stitching because the special coating can rub off on the tension discs and gum up the machine.

Key feature
Coated for stretch and to resist tangling

Common uses
Hand stitching and hand quilting

Fabric type
Wovens

Needle type
Sharps and betweens

DECORATIVE: EMBROIDERY

Embroidery thread is made from rayon or viscose and is used for machine embroidery, decorative stitches, satin stitches and smocking. It is very shiny, smooth and lustrous and makes an affordable alternative to silk thread. It comes in both solid and variegated colours. Embroidery thread is used in the needle while all-purpose thread is used in the bobbin.

Key feature
Shiny and smooth

Common uses
Decorative stitches, embroidery and smocking

Fabric type
Wovens and knits

Needle type
Embroidery

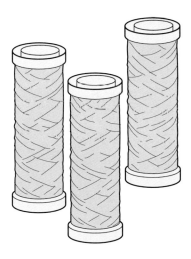

DECORATIVE: METALLIC

Metallic thread adds sparkle and glitz and is used for machine embroidery, satin stitches and decorative stitching. It has a polyester, nylon or rayon core that is wrapped in metallic fibres and films. Metallic threads can shred, fray and break easily so stitch slowly to protect them.

Key feature
Sparkly

Common uses
Decorative stitches and embroidery

Fabric type
Wovens and knits

Needle type
Metallic

 EXPERT TIP Thread deteriorates with age and becomes brittle, so avoid old thread on wooden spools. Also, don't use discount thread because it tends to tangle and break easily. Thread needs to be strong and smooth enough to move through a sewing machine at high speeds without snapping or tangling.

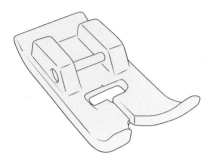

ALL-PURPOSE FOOT

The all-purpose foot is also known as the zigzag foot. It has a wide hole to allow the needle to swing left and right and is intended for stitches that have width but is also used for straight stitching. Use the all-purpose foot when using a twin needle or when adjusting the needle position right or left of centre. A small groove on the bottom allows for the build-up of stitches when doing decorative stitching.

Key feature
Wide hole

Common uses
General purpose

Fabric type
All

Thread type
All

Needle type
All

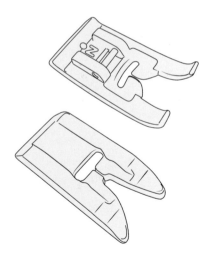

SATIN STITCH FOOT

This is like the all-purpose foot except it has a deep groove on the bottom to accommodate the build-up of heavy satin stitches or decorative embroidery stitches. It is often made from plastic to allow improved visibility. It has a well-defined centre front mark to use as a seam guide.

Key feature
Deep groove on bottom

Common uses
Satin stitches, decorative stitches and appliqué

Fabric type
All

Thread type
All

Needle type
All

 EXPERT TIP Some sewing machines come with a built-in even-feed mechanism. Pushing a button on the shank engages a set of upper feed dogs.

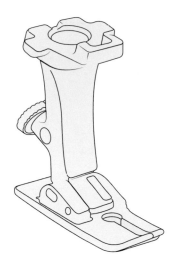

STRAIGHT STITCH FOOT

The straight stitch foot has a small hole in the centre and is used exclusively for straight stitching with the needle in the centre position. The hole design supports the fabric and prevents the needle from pushing lightweight fabrics into the needle hole. The bottom of the foot is very smooth to allow maximum contact with the feed dogs for even stitches.

Key feature
Small hole

Common uses
Seams, piecing, topstitching and darts

Fabric type
All

Thread type
All

Needle type
Universal, quilting, ballpoint, stretch, Microtex, denim, topstitch, leather, embroidery or metallic

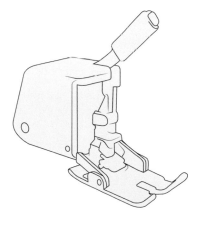

WALKING FOOT/EVEN FEED FOOT

The walking foot has an upper set of feed dogs to feed the top layer of fabric at the same speed as the bottom layer. It is used when precision sewing is essential and for fabrics that are difficult to feed. The wide needle hole allows for zigzag stitches and twin needles, and a slot on the back allows you to insert a quilt bar.

Key feature
Upper set of feed dogs to help fabric layers feed evenly

Common uses
Quilting, seaming plaids and stripes, difficult fabrics such as leather, knits and faux fur

Fabric type
All

Thread type
Cotton or polyester

Needle type
All

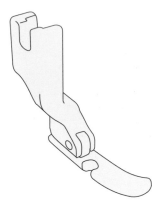

ZIPPER FOOT

The zipper foot is narrow with a small notch on either side to allow the needle to stitch very close to the zipper coils or teeth. It is used for stitching on all types of zippers. It will either be snap-on and can be manually attached to either side or will have a screw to slide it left or right.

Key feature
Narrow with a small notch on either side

Common uses
Zippers and piping

Fabric type
All

Thread type
Cotton or polyester

Needle type
Universal, Microtex or denim

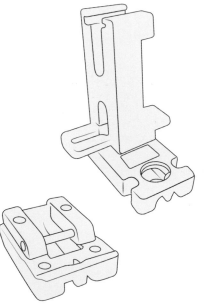

INVISIBLE ZIPPER FOOT

The invisible zipper foot is used exclusively for stitching on invisible zippers and has two grooves on the bottom of the foot that the zipper coils fit into. It allows you to stitch incredibly close to the zipper coil without stitching through it. If you cannot find an invisible zipper foot for your machine, you can purchase a universal kit at any fabric store with a plastic invisible zipper foot as well as shanks that should fit any machine.

Key feature
Two deep grooves on bottom

Common uses
Invisible zippers

Fabric type
All

Thread type
Cotton or polyester

Needle type
Universal, Microtex or denim

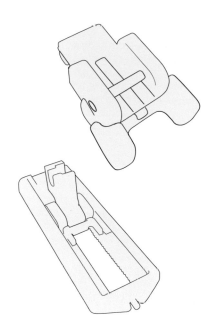

BUTTONHOLE FOOT

A manual buttonhole is used for 4-step basic buttonholes and has an adjustable window and markings to help align and size buttonholes. Twin grooves on the bottom of the foot accommodate the dense stitches and a back hook and front fork hold cording for corded buttonholes. On sewing machines that do a 1-step buttonhole, an automatic buttonhole foot can be used for basic, keyhole, stretch and bound buttonholes. It has an extension on the back where you insert the button you are using. The machine automatically sizes the buttonhole to fit that button.

Key feature
Deep groove on bottom

Common uses
Buttonholes

Fabric type
All

Thread type
Cotton, polyester or embroidery

Needle type
Universal, Microtex or embroidery

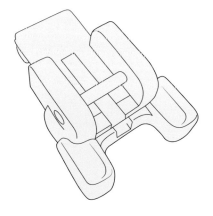

BUTTON FOOT

Button feet have two very short, widely spaced toes. They anchor a sew-through button in place while you stitch it down. They cannot be used on shank buttons. Some button feet have a slot to insert a pin or toothpick to create a thread shank. They can also be used to stitch on sew-through snaps and hooks and eyes.

Key feature
Two short toes coated with rubber

Common uses
Buttons, snaps, and hooks and eyes

Fabric type
All

Thread type
Cotton, polyester or topstitch

Needle type
Universal or topstitch

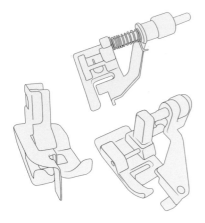

BLIND HEM FOOT

The blind hem foot has an adjustable bar that you can move next to a fold of fabric when stitching blind hems. Other blind hem feet have a fixed metal guide in the centre. You may need to adjust the needle position setting on your machine when using this type of blind hem foot. You can also use the blind hem foot for topstitching, edgestitching and decorative stitching.

Key feature
Adjustable or fixed guide bar

Common uses
Blind hems, topstitching, edgestitching and decorative stitching

Fabric type
All

Thread type
Cotton or polyester

Needle type
Universal or Microtex

OVERCAST FOOT

The overcast foot has a small pin or finger that holds the fabric edges down flat to prevent them from curling under and a blade to the right to act as a seam guide. The needle will zigzag over the pin and the right side of the zigzag will go off the edge of the fabric. It is used for all types of overcasting seam finishes to prevent fabrics from fraying and for stitches that seam and finish in one operation. Never use a straight stitch or any stitch where the needle will hit the centre pin or the needle will break.

Key feature
Pin to hold fabric edge down

Common uses
Seam finishes and overcasting

Fabric type
All

Thread type
Cotton or polyester

Needle type
Universal, Microtex, stretch or ballpoint

PATCHWORK FOOT

The patchwork foot, also called a piecing or ¼in foot, has a narrow right toe with a guide 6mm (¹/₄in) from the centre needle position. It may also have a 3mm (¹/₈in) marking on the right toe and 6mm (¹/₄in) and 3mm (¹/₈in) markings on the sides for perfectly placed pivot turns. This is used for piecing quilt tops, patchwork, topstitching and any situation where perfect 6mm (¹/₄in) seams are needed.

Key feature
Narrow right side that is 6mm (¹/₄in) wide

Common uses
Piecing quilt tops and topstitching

Fabric type
All

Thread type
Cotton, polyester or topstitch

Needle type
Universal, Microtex, topstitching or leather

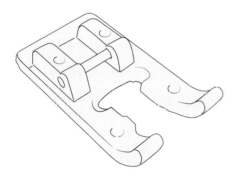

OPEN TOE FOOT

The open toe foot provides an unobstructed view while sewing and the long toes provide good traction against the feed dogs. It is used for appliqué, smocking, satin stitching, heirloom and other decorative stitches. It is commonly clear plastic and has a groove to permit dense stitches to pass underneath it.

Key feature
Long toes with open space between

Common uses
Smocking, satin stitches and decorative stitches

Fabric type
All

Thread type
Cotton, polyester, embroidery or metallic

Needle type
Universal, Microtex, embroidery, wing or metallic

Computerised Sewing Machines

Computerised sewing machines have circuits and computer chips inside to control the operations of the machine such as needle movement and feed-dog movement. They also have push buttons, keypads or touch screens to adjust stitch selection, length, and width. Most computerised machines have a digital display that shows what the stitch looks like, which presser foot should be used with that stitch, and even a recommended needle type.

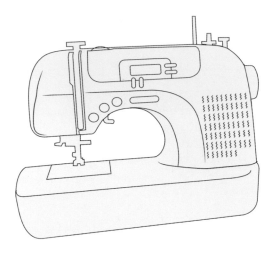

HOW TO CHANGE STITCHES AND SETTINGS ON A COMPUTERISED MACHINE

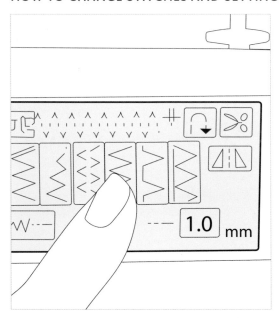

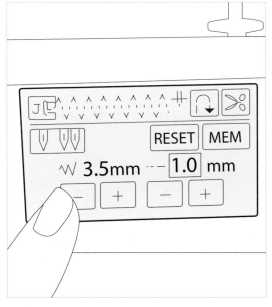

1 Select the desired stitch by pushing a button, touching the screen or entering a stitch number.

2 Check the stitch length and width and adjust as needed. Make sure the correct presser foot and needle are installed.

STITCH LENGTH AND WIDTH

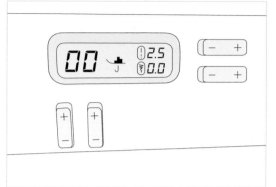

Most machines can do a stitch length up to 5mm but some go up to 9mm long. Standard stitch width is 4mm but some have wider widths up to 7mm and wider needle holes for a wider stitch width. One of the benefits of a computerised machine is that when a stitch pattern is selected, the stitch length and width will adjust automatically to the standard option for that particular stitch. But you can always fine-tune the stitch length and stitch width as desired by pushing a button or touching the touchscreen.

OTHER FEATURES

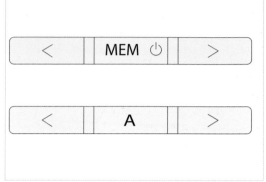

Many have a memory function that allows you to store a particular stitch with preferred settings so that it is easy to use it again on a future project. Imagine storing a buttonhole style and length and then stitching an identical buttonhole a month later! Many also have the capability to start and stop a stitch at a certain point in the stitch sequence. This is very useful with decorative stitches when you don't want a partially finished motif. Often there is an option to bypass the foot pedal and you can sew by simply pushing the start button. Many models have powerful editing capabilities so you can enlarge, rotate and mirror image a design.

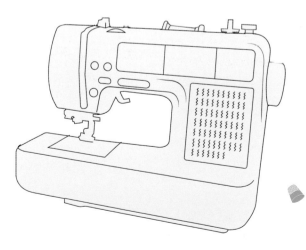

EXPERT TIP Be careful when using a magnetic pin cushion near a computerised sewing machine. Every sewing machine manufacturer has different guidelines for this but it's best to err on the side of caution and keep magnets as far away as possible from computerised machines.

Mechanical sewing machines have gears, cams, drive shafts and belts inside, all of which are powered by a single electric motor. They also have dials, levers or sliders to adjust stitch pattern, length and width. The motor is controlled by the foot pedal; when the foot pedal is pressed, the motor drives all of the processes at a synchronized rate.

STITCH PATTERN

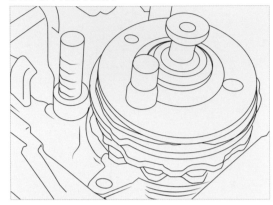

These machines have internal and permanent cams that are stacked. A cam is a plastic or metal disc with indentations around the circumference. Each cam is notched slightly differently and is for a specific stitch pattern. As the machine operates, a finger follows the shape of the cam and that is what moves the needle bar for that stitch. Since the cams are built-in, additional stitches cannot be added.

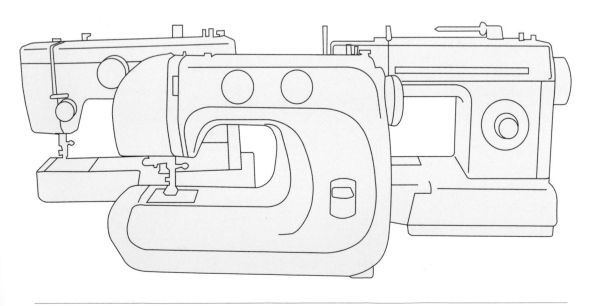

STITCH LENGTH AND WIDTH

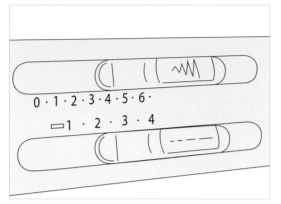

Most mechanical machines can do a stitch length up to 4mm but some go up to 5mm long. Standard stitch width is 4mm. Mechanical sewing machines must have the settings manually adjusted. So if the zigzag stitch is selected, the stitch width must be adjusted from 0mm to the desired width or else it is still a straight stitch.

OTHER FEATURES

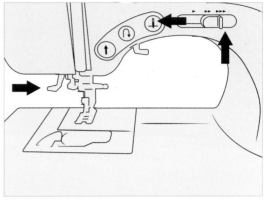

Some mechanical machines have bonus features such as needle up and down, speed control and an automatic needle threader.

HOW TO CHANGE STITCHES AND SETTINGS ON A MECHANICAL MACHINE

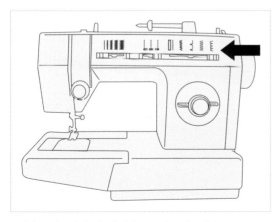

1 Select the desired stitch by turning the dial or adjusting the lever or slider

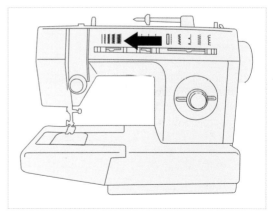

2 Check the stitch length and width and adjust as needed. Make sure the correct presser foot and needle are installed.

 EXPERT TIP Never change stitch pattern or width while the needle is in the fabric or the needle may break.

Vintage Sewing Machine with Cams

Many vintage sewing machines from the 1950s and 1960s have external cams that are required when stitching anything other than basic straight stitch. Since they are mechanical machines, they have dials, levers or sliders to adjust all the settings such as stitch length and width.

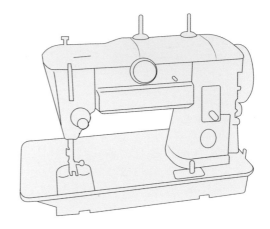

STITCH PATTERN

The cams are needed to create utility and decorative stitches. When the cam is inserted in the sewing machine, the 'bumps' make the needle move left or right to form the stitches. Each different cam makes the sewing machine form one specific decorative stitch. These machines were sold with some basic cams and then additional cams were sold separately so you could add stitches to the machine as your skills and budget allowed. The cams are inserted into the top on most machines but sometimes are inserted on the back. Most vintage sewing machines have a maximum stitch length of 4mm and stitch width of 4mm. The length and width settings must be manually adjusted for the different stitches.

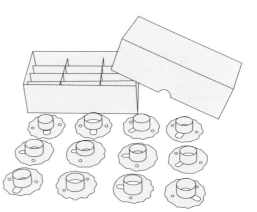

HOW TO CHANGE STITCHES AND SETTINGS ON A VINTAGE MACHINE

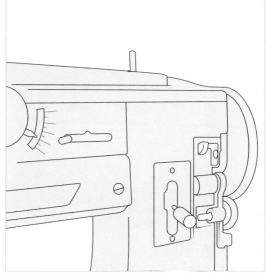

1 Open the top of the machine. Insert the cam for the desired stitch on the spindle and snap in place. To remove the cam, check for a release lever. On other machines, you simply pull on the cam to remove it.

2 Check the stitch length and width and adjust as needed. Make sure the correct presser foot and needle are installed.

 EXPERT TIP Many vintage sewing machines are sold without the cams. You can usually find individual cams or complete sets on eBay.

Glossary

APPLIQUÉ
A technique in which a piece of fabric is sewn on top of another piece of fabric.

BACKTACK
Reverse stitches at the beginning and end of a hand-stitched seam used to secure the threads and prevent the seam from coming undone. On machine sewing this is called backstitching.

BIAS GRAIN
The 45-degree angle on fabric between the length and cross grain. Fabrics stretch on the bias.

BINDING
A narrow strip of fabric cut on the bias or cross grain to give stretch and wrapped around an edge to finish it neatly. It is used on necklines, armholes, hems and quilts.

CROSS GRAIN
On a fabric weave, the threads that run from selvedge to selvedge. Also known as the weft.

DART
A stitched fold of fabric used to shape garments. They are often seen at the waist or bust.

EASE
The extra room in a garment to allow for movement and comfort.

EDGESTITCH
Stitching very close to an edge or seam line. It is usually 3mm (1/8in) or less.

FACING
A piece of fabric sewn to an edge and turned to the inside to conceal seam allowances and finish edges.

FEED DOG
The teeth under the needle plate on a sewing machine that move the fabric as the needle makes the stitch.

GRAINLINE
Usually refers to the direction of threads in fabric but also refers to the printed grainline on a pattern.

HEM ALLOWANCE
The total amount of fabric included on a pattern for a hem.

INTERFACING
A material used to stiffen, strengthen or stabilise another fabric. It can fused on or sewn in.

LENGTH GRAIN
On a fabric weave, the threads that are parallel to the selvedge. Also known as the warp.

NAP
The raised surface on a fabric such as velvet where all the fibres are pointing in one direction. Napped fabrics must be cut as a one-way layout. Fabrics with a one-way print must follow a napped layout.

OVERCAST
A seam-finishing stitch where the thread wraps over the raw edge.

PINKING
A seam finishing technique using pinking shears that make zigzag cuts on the edge to prevent fraying.

PIVOT
A technique to stitch corners where you lower the needle in the fabric, lift the presser foot, and turn the fabric around the needle.

PRESSER FOOT
Holds fabric down against the feed dog unit so it can move under the needle. Some are basic and some are for specialty applications.

RAW EDGE
The unfinished cut edge of a piece of fabric.

RIGHT SIDE

The side of fabric that will be visible from the outside of a finished project. Often abbreviated to RS.

SATIN STITCH

Zigzag stitches that are very closely spaced. They are used as embroidery, for monograms and for stitching on appliqués.

SEAM

A line of stitches that joins two pieces of fabric.

SEAM ALLOWANCE

The distance between a seam and the raw edge. Most patterns have seam allowances included and they are usually 15mm (5/8in).

SEAM FINISH

A technique to prevent the raw edge of a fabric from fraying and ravelling. Common seam finishes are pinking, zigzag, binding and serging.

SELVEDGES

The finished edges down either side of a length of fabric. They are frequently printed with manufacturer's information and are more tightly woven than the rest of the fabric.

SERGE

The chain stitch produced by a serger or overlock machine. Can be used as a construction seam or seam finish.

SHANK

Attaches a presser foot to a sewing machine. Machines are designed for low shank, high shank or slant shank. Some feet are attached to a shank and some snap on to a shank.

STAY STITCH

A line of stitches used to stabilise an edge and prevent it from stretching.

TACKING

A temporary seam using very long stitches. It can be done by hand or by machine. Tacking stitches are removed when they are no longer needed.

TAILOR'S HAM

A pressing tool that is used for pressing curved seams and darts without distorting them. One side is covered in wool and the other is covered in cotton and it is stuffed with sawdust.

TOPSTITCH

Stitching close to an edge or seam line, usually 6mm (1/4in) from the edge.

WARP

On a fabric weave, the threads that are parallel to the selvedge. Also known as the length grain.

WEFT

On a fabric weave, the threads that run from selvedge to selvedge. Also known as the cross grain.

WRONG SIDE

The side of fabric that will not be seen on the outside of a finished project. Often abbreviated to WS.

Further Reading

ONLINE SUPPLIERS

Bolt
boltfabricboutique.com

Britex
britexfabrics.com

Cool Cottons
coolcottons.biz

Denver Fabrics
denverfabrics.com

Etsy
etsy.com

F & S Fabrics
fandsfabrics.com

Fabric.com
fabric.com

Fashion Fabrics Club
fashionfabricsclub.com

Gorgeous Fabrics
gorgeousfabrics.com

Harts Fabrics
hartsfabric.com

International Silks and Woolens
internationalsilks.com

Liberty
liberty.co.uk

Manhattan Fabrics
manhattanfabrics.com

Michael Levine
mlfabric.com

Mood Fabrics
moodfabrics.com

Paron Fabrics
paronfabrics.com

Robert Kaufman Fabrics
robertkaufman.com

Sew Mama Sew
sewmamasew.com

Stonemountain and Daughter Fabrics
stonemountainfabric.com

Vogue Fabrics
voguefabricsstore.com

Westminster Fabrics
westminsterfabrics.com

WEBSITES AND BLOGS

A Fashionable Stitch
afashionablestitch.com
Authentic handmade style and fashion

American Sewing Guild
asg.org
A membership organisation for sewing enthusiasts

Burda Style
burdastyle.com
Projects and patterns for sewists

CRAFT
craftzine.com
Transforming traditional crafts

Collete Patterns Blog
coletterie.com
Sewing tips, ideas and peeks

Gertie's Blog for Better Sewing
blogforbettersewing.com
A homage to Vogue's 1952 better sewing book

MADE
dana-made-it.com
Includes clothing tutorials

Pattern Review
sewing.patternreview.com
Includes many shop patterns

BOOKS

Chic and Simple Sewing, by Christine Haynes.
Potter Craft, 2009.

Claire Shaeffer's Fabric Sewing Guide, by Claire Shaeffer.
Krause Publications, 2008.

Complete Embellishing: Techniques and Projects,
by Kayte Terry. Creative Homeowner, 2008.

Fast Fit Easy Pattern Alterations for Every Figure,
by Sandra Betzina. Taunton Press, 2004.

Fit for Real People, by Pati Palmer and Marta Alto.
Palmer-Pletsch Associates, 2006.

Sew Everything Workshop, by Diana Rupp.
Workman Publishing, 2007.

Sew U Home Stretch, by Wendy Mullin.
Little Brown Book Group, 2008.

Sewing Machine Secrets, by Nicole Vasbinder.
Interweave, 2013.

Stress Free Sewing, by Nicole Vasbinder.
Interweave, 2012.

The New Sewing with a Serger, Singer Photo Reference
Library. Creative Publishing International, 1999.

*The Vogue/Butterick Step-By-Step Guide to Sewing
Techniques*, by the editors of Vogue and Butterick
Patterns. Sixth & Spring Books, 2012.

MAGAZINES

Sew Stylish
craftstylish.com/sewstylish
Includes fashion, restyle and sewing

Stitch
sewdaily.com/blogs/stitchblog/pages/about-stitch.aspx
A quarterly sewing magazine all about creating with
fabric and thread

Threads
threadsmagazine.com
Magazine for sewing enthusiasts, including garments

Index

Acknowledgements

It was a pleasure to work with the team at RotoVision on this book. Thank you to Cath Senker and Lindy Dunlop for editing all the text, keeping me on track, and making sure that all my explanations and tutorials made sense. Thank you to Isheeta Mustafi for approaching me to write this book and being so patient as we worked through the concepts.

Once again it was a joy to work with Sherry Heck. Her beautiful photographs bring a level of artistry to all of these projects and I'm so glad she brought in Heather Sanksy to style the photographs so charmingly!

Thank you so much to all of the people who have taken a sewing class with me over the years. I have learned so much from my students because their questions force me to think of new ways to explain things. It's been a blast while writing this book and showing my students all these stitches and seeing how excited they get as they master new skills and explore their machines.

Thanks to my family and friends for understanding as I disappeared for weeks while doing research. Thank you to my mum for buying me my first sewing machine and always being my biggest cheerleader.

And finally, thank you especially to my husband Vince. You are my rock and I love you. This book is dedicated to you.